Two Jewish Justices

Robert A. Burt

Two Jewish Justices

Outcasts in the Promised Land

University of California Press
Berkeley Los Angeles London

Many people have helped me in writing this book and I am grateful, in particular, to Linda Burt, Bruce Ackerman, Aharon Barak, Lee Bollinger, Fred Busch, Norman Dorsen, Charles Halpern, Susan Halpern, Jay Katz, Robert Post, Michael Paul Rogin, Mark Rose, Catherine Ross, Paul Schwartz, Alan Weisbard, Jack Weinstein and, for her invaluable editing and research assistance, Jean Fraser.

University of California Press
Berkeley and Los Angeles, California

University of California Press, Ltd.
London, England

Library of Congress Cataloging-in-Publication Data

Burt, Robert, 1939-
Two Jewish justices.

Includes bibliographical references and index.
1. Brandeis, Louis Dembitz, 1856–1941.
2. Frankfurter, Felix, 1882–1965. 3. Jewish judges—United States—Biography. 4. Judges—United States—Biography.
I. Title.
KF8744.B87 1988 347.73'14'089924 87–19161
347.30714089924
ISBN 0–520–06110–1 (alk. paper)

Printed in the United States of America
1 2 3 4 5 6 7 8 9

To Anne,
To Jessica, and
To the memory of my father

Contents

1

Diaspora Jew

When I arrived at the Yale Law School as a student in 1962, I felt somehow that I had found a home. One possible explanation for this occurred to me: that there were a considerable number of Jews among my classmates, many more in numbers and in proportion than in my college or previous public school experience. I had been bar mitzvahed, like all of my Jewish male friends, and had belonged to a Jewish fraternity in high school; but I was not then, nor am I now, a religiously observant Jew. Until coming to Yale Law School, I had not noticed any absence of Jews around me. Though I made no precise count at Yale, it seemed to me that almost half my law school classmates were Jews; and I was startled by this sudden experience of being so much surrounded by Jews in a place other than a synagogue. There seemed, however, so many other reasons that I felt at home in law school that I set this one impression aside at the time.

In 1968 I began law teaching and felt almost at once that this career choice was the right one for me. Once again I noticed the considerable concentration of Jews among my teaching colleagues, a markedly higher proportion than in the world of law practice. When I returned to Yale in 1976 as a law school faculty member, I was particularly struck by the fact that almost half my colleagues here were Jewish. I discussed this with a few friends; we all agreed—it was a commonplace observation—on the relevance of the Jewish talmudic tradition and the special reliance by our parents and grandparents on professional education as a vehicle for assimilation in America. I thought little more about the matter.

Three years ago my friend and law school classmate Charles Halpern, now dean of the City University of New York Law School, asked me to give a lecture as part of a program in honor of his father at his family's synagogue in Buffalo. The appointed subject, Charlie told me, was the role of Jews in American law.[1] This book grew from that invitation. I took the occasion to read and to think in a sustained way about the impressions I had carried with me for many years—to try to understand why I and so many other Jews of my generation have found a home in America as lawyers, and in particular as law teachers.

I began by considering the careers of Louis Brandeis and Felix Frankfurter—two Jews who attained great prominence at a time when the American legal profession generally was inhospitable to Jews. I read through their opinions, their biographies, their extrajudicial writings, and other sources, trying to discern what role their Jewishness played in their conception of themselves as people and as Supreme Court justices.[2] I concluded, as I set out in the first two chapters of this book, that Jewishness was distinctively associated with outsider status, with homelessness, for both Brandeis and Frankfurter. I further found that the two men gave conflicting valuations to this status and to their Jewishness both in their personal lives and in their conduct as Supreme Court justices.

The example of these two men did not immediately translate, however, into an understanding of the contemporary role of Jews in the legal profession. In particular, as my own experience indicates, Jews today are much more welcome in the profession than in Brandeis's or Frankfurter's times. I came, then, to a further set of questions: what characteristics of contemporary American society might explain its unprecedented hospitality to Jews in the legal profession generally, and in law teaching specifically? This inquiry led me to speculate about the status of other minorities, such as blacks, disabled people, and women, in this country; and most particularly about the significance for American culture of black slavery, Jim Crow and the second Reconstruction in our time, and the possible parallels with the experience of European Jews in the nineteenth and twentieth centuries.

From these speculations, I came to the conclusion that outsider status, homelessness, is pervasively experienced in American society today—not simply among those groups customarily conceived in this way, such as blacks or Jews, but generally; and that this generalized experience both explains the easier contemporary acceptance of Jews in America and points to possible future dangers for Jews, for blacks, for other minorities, for all Americans. Following these considerations, I found contemporary meaning in the examples set by Brandeis and Frankfurter as distinctively Jewish justices. I came to see, that is, that their different attitudes toward outsider status and homelessness have direct relevance to the issues confronted today by all judges in America, and by all Americans, whether Jews or gentiles. I develop all of this in the succeeding three chapters of this book.

As this quick summary indicates, my account is both speculative and selective in its emphasis. I am not presenting a comprehensive study of the life or the jurisprudence of Brandeis or Frankfurter. I have intentionally narrowed my focus to specific aspects of their lives and specific judicial decisions that illuminate the one theme I am pursuing. I do believe that my account is not contradicted by other aspects of their lives or other decisions that I do not discuss here; but I do not undertake to prove this proposition by exhaustive citation.

I am also narrowly selective in my account of the significance of Jewishness in American life. Indeed, there are three other Jewish justices—Benjamin Cardozo, Arthur Goldberg, and Abe Fortas—and many other Jewish judges whom I do not directly consider.[3] The theme I have identified does, I believe, have some relevance to the experience of all of these men; as I have said, I am bold enough to claim that this theme casts some light on the contemporary status of all Americans. I have thus addressed a broad range of questions in a narrowly focused inquiry. I hope that the very constriction of my focus will provide an intensified illumination of the truth in this one theme.

In my reading about the status of Jews in American law, I encountered an example that seemed to epitomize this central theme: Judah P. Benjamin, whose name President Millard Fillmore sent to the Senate for confirmation as a Supreme Court justice in 1853. Benjamin would have been the first Jewish justice, but he declined the nomination.

If Judah Benjamin had not existed as the first-nominated Jewish justice, however, I would be tempted to invent him. Consider his career both before and after he was offered this place in the pantheon of American Jewish heroes.[4] Benjamin was born a British subject in 1811 on the island of St. Croix in the West Indies. He was raised in North Carolina, attended Yale College, and spent his early career as an attorney in New Orleans. In 1852 he was elected United States senator from Louisiana. Benjamin remained in the Senate until secession in 1861, when he withdrew with his Southern colleagues; he then served successively as attorney general, secretary of war, and secretary of state of the Confederacy. When the war was lost, in order to avoid capture and trial for treason, Benjamin disguised himself as a Frenchman and escaped to England. Now embracing his third homeland, Benjamin became an outstandingly successful barrister. When he died in 1884, his extensive obituary in *The Times* of London included this observation:

> His life was as various as an Eastern tale, and he carved out for himself by his own unaided exertions, not one

> but three several histories. . . . No less inherited is that elastic resistance to evil fortune which preserved Mr. Benjamin's ancestors through a succession of exiles and plunderings, and reappeared in the Minister of the Confederate cause.

The "Eastern tale" of this first-nominated Jewish justice anticipates the central theme of the stories that follow. In the span of his life, Judah Benjamin held three nationalities (four, if his brief masquerade as a Frenchman is counted). He was a paradigmatic diaspora Jew, a survivor whose homeless wanderings were essential to his survival. Benjamin's quest for a home, some secure resting place, was reiterated in different ways and with different results by Brandeis and Frankfurter. This quest has yet a different significance in our generation, for Jews and for gentiles. That is the subject of this book.

2

Brandeis

Louis Dembitz Brandeis is the founding father of the Jewish presence in American law—not only the first Jew to serve as a justice of the United States Supreme Court but also, if not the first, then among the first to be offered a faculty appointment at that other pinnacle of respectability in American law, the Harvard Law School (an offer he declined).[1] The status of Jews in America is, however, different today from what it was in Brandeis's time; and Jews' status also changed between 1882, when Harvard called Brandeis, and 1916, when President Woodrow Wilson nominated him to the Court.

When the Harvard appointment was offered to Brandeis, there were between three and four hundred thousand Jews in America.[2] All but some fifty thousand of these had come to this country during the preceding thirty years, since 1850; most of these immigrants, like Brandeis's family, were of German origin. But for the most part even these recent immigrants wore their Jewishness lightly. They had not seen themselves as radically separated from German gentile society; in their own vision, they were part of German culture, though they acknowledged the existence and force of anti-Semitic feeling that barred them from fully assimilated status.[3]

Brandeis's family was typical in this regard.[4] They were financially secure and well educated. Though they emigrated following the failure of the 1848 revolution, when many other

German Jews also left for America in response to heightened anti-Semitism, the Brandeis clan did not seek out other Jews in this country. They settled together, not as Jews but as an extended family of brothers, sisters, and cousins, in Kentucky, where they quickly established cordial and financially prosperous relations with their gentile neighbors. Louis was born in 1856 into this essentially assimilated setting; his Jewishness was not denied, but it was not observed at his home in any way. Thus Louis could associate with others almost without Jewish self-consciousness as such. This seems to have been his attitude and the reciprocated attitude of his fellow students at Harvard Law School in the 1870s, where he performed brilliantly; his Jewishness played no discernible role in Harvard's subsequent decision to extend a teaching offer to him.[5]

But by 1916, when he was nominated to the Court, anti-Semitism had become a palpable force in American life and Brandeis's Jewishness was very much an issue.[6] By that time, the character of the Jewish population in America had been transformed. Almost two million Jews had arrived since 1880; and most of them came from the rigidly segregated shtetels of eastern Europe.[7] The new Jewish immigrants were not equipped by social experience or formal education to pursue assimilationist ambitions in American society with the easy grace of the Brandeis family and other earlier German Jewish immigrants.

By 1916, moreover, Louis Brandeis's attitude toward his own Jewishness had itself been transformed. Though his great professional and financial success as a Boston attorney might have underwritten his assimilated status and confirmed his essentially secular social identity, this was not Brandeis's path. By 1916 Brandeis had become a passionate Zionist, and not in a small or quiet way. He was the acknowledged leader of the American Zionist Organization, the chairman of its Executive Committee.[8] But there was a puzzle here. Brandeis had come to Zionism only a few years earlier. Before that time he had not been involved in Zionism or in Jewish communal affairs. As he himself admitted in his speech accepting the chairmanship of the American organization: "I have been to a great extent separated from Jews. I am very ignorant in things Jewish."[9]

The American Zionists' embrace of Brandeis as their leader is easier to understand than his acceptance of that role.[10] For the Zionists, Brandeis represented a social coup. He was by then perhaps the best-known private attorney in the United States, a confidant of President Wilson's, and a visibly successful member of the German-American-Jewish community, who, almost without exception, kept a scornful distance from their eastern European coreligionists generally, and from Zionism in particular. Zionism, moreover, had achieved only limited success in attracting adherents among the recent Jewish immigrants from eastern Europe, who were eager to assimilate in all things American and, indeed, viewed America itself as their new Zion. Brandeis gave respectability, the seal of American assimilation, to Zionism. The American Zionists were happy to have him, if not a little incredulous; and they expected him to be a figurehead chairman.[11]

But they had not reckoned with Brandeis's capacious energy or with the depth of his commitment notwithstanding the recency of his conversion to Zionism and, one might even say, to Judaism. So deep was this commitment that when Brandeis was confirmed to the Court, he resigned all extrajudicial affiliations (and there were many: he was a prodigious joiner in civic affairs) except for his involvement in the Zionist movement.[12] Moreover, in 1920 he seriously considered resigning from the Court in order to assume the proffered leadership of the World Zionist Organization.[13] And, near the end of his life, he told his authorized biographer, Alpheus Thomas Mason, that Zionism, more than any other cause in his life, had fired his imagination and captured his heart.[14]

What explains his latter-day conversion and its abiding intensity for Brandeis? From my reading of his life and his character, I would offer one explanation: that throughout his life, Brandeis saw himself standing alone at the margin of his society. Though he had many opportunities to deny this, to find some comfortable communal affiliation and an "insider's" status, Brandeis always turned away; he always found a place to stand alone.

This solitary stance was a defining characteristic of virtually every facet of Brandeis's life. Consider, for example, Brandeis's definition of his professional role as an attorney. The clearest statement of his role definition came in an attack on him, as the fundamental reason why he was unfit to serve on the Supreme Court. Speaking on behalf of seven past presidents of the American Bar Association and fifty-seven of the most prominent lawyers and other citizens in Boston, where Brandeis practiced, the leader of this opposition said this in Senate hearings to oppose his confirmation: "Mr. Brandeis does not act according to the canons of the Bar. The trouble with Mr. Brandeis is that he . . . always acts the part of a judge toward his clients, instead of being his client's lawyer, which is against the practices of the Bar."[15]

This may seem an extraordinary basis on which to find a person unfit for judicial office. But the charge was seriously meant: that Brandeis violated professional norms because he insisted on applying his own standards of right conduct to his clients and therefore was prepared to judge them before he would undertake advocacy on their behalf.[16] In this stance, Brandeis not only stood outside the conventional professional norms of his day; he stood apart from, and maintained a critical distance from, his clients.

Brandeis acted on this independent conception of an attorney's role not only in his dealings with specific clients but more generally. In an address delivered in 1905, he observed:

> The leading lawyers of the United States have been engaged mainly in supporting the claims of the corpora-

> tions. . . . Instead of holding a position of independence, between the wealthy and the people, prepared to curb the excesses of either, able lawyers have, to a large extent, allowed themselves to become adjuncts of great corporations and have neglected the obligation to use their powers for the protection of the people. . . . We hear much of the "corporation lawyer," and far too little of the "people's lawyer."[17]

Brandeis himself became widely known as the "people's lawyer" because of his (always unpaid) advocacy of consumer interests in a wide variety of causes—municipal railway monopolization, life insurance practices, public land conservation, and the like.[18] But note in Brandeis's description of his role the characteristic insistence on his independence; he did not see himself invariably as the champion of the people against the few, the poor against the wealthy. He stood apart from both sides, always prepared, as he saw it, "to curb the excesses of either."

There is a problematic aspect to this role conception, an extraordinary self-confidence in one's own rectitude and disinterestedness. But I do not intend to explore this problem critically for my purposes here; I want simply to identify the force of this conception of professional independence, this stance alone and apart, for Brandeis.

Brandeis himself spoke of this self-conception in his most enduring judicial opinion, his dissent in *Olmstead v. United States*.[19] The "makers of our Constitution," he claimed, "recognized the significance of man's spiritual nature, of his feelings and of his intellect. . . . They conferred, as against the Government, the right to be let alone—the most comprehensive of rights and the right most valued by civilized men." Brandeis wrote this in 1928, when he was seventy-one years old. Almost forty years earlier, when he was just thirty-four, he had published virtually the same words in a *Harvard Law*

Review article on the right to privacy, written with his law partner, Samuel Warren:

> In very early times, the [common] law gave a remedy only for physical interference with life and property. . . . Later, there came a recognition of man's spiritual nature, of his feelings and his intellect. Gradually the scope of these legal rights broadened; and now the right to life has come to mean the right to enjoy life,—the right to be let alone.[20]

Though the words were the same, the context for them differed. In his *Olmstead* opinion, Brandeis asserted this privacy right against government intrusions (telephone wiretapping, to be specific); in his article with Warren, the claim was against newspaper publicists serving "idle or prurient [public] curiosity."[21] But in both contexts, the underlying goal Brandeis sought was the same, as he clearly articulated in the *Harvard* article: "The intensity and complexity of life, attendant upon advancing civilization, have rendered necessary some retreat from the world. . . . [S]olitude and privacy have become more essential to the individual."[22]

This prized solitude, this embrace of "some retreat from the world," is at the heart of Brandeis's lifelong stance alone and apart. Brandeis's conception and his high valuation of the solitary individual had pervasive significance for him. He drew his overarching political ideal for American society from this intensely individualist stance; it was the basis for his excoriation of the "curse of bigness," the increasingly far-flung scale and complexity that he saw in American economic and social life.[23]

Brandeis's high valuation of solitude also found expression in his personal attributes. His social presence was characterized, as one close observer put it, by "silence and reserve and impersonalness." This was the description offered by Dean

Acheson in 1920 during his service as Brandeis's third law clerk; Acheson wrote this in a letter to his former teacher, Felix Frankfurter, attempting to identify the components of Brandeis's "greatness."[24] For Acheson, these personal characteristics were admirable; but they were not necessarily so for all Brandeis's clerks. Imagine the interpersonal relations between justice and law clerk implied in this anecdote, recounted in a recent biography of Brandeis:

> A number of clerks report the experience of working through the night in the upstairs office [above Brandeis's own apartment] on a memorandum or opinion the justice particularly wanted. Each tiptoed to the front door of the justice's residence at about 5:30 in the morning and slipped his papers partway under the door, only to watch as a mysterious hand pulled the papers from the other side.[25]

Is it not striking that Brandeis would not open the door to greet, even perhaps to thank, his hard-working clerk? The vignette is small, of course; but it captures an attribute that can be gleaned from numerous accounts of Brandeis's social interactions, and not only with his subordinates. Thus Alpheus Thomas Mason notes that time spent with his law clients was "carefully budgeted": "Every conference [with clients] was speeded up—so much so that one client remarked that he could not stay in Brandeis's office except by clinging to some substantial object. The office itself was furnished with austerity. There was no rug or easy chair. The temperature was kept so low that in winter the client could be comfortable only by keeping on his overcoat."[26] And consider this observation from a peer and an admirer. Justice Oliver Wendell Holmes, who was Brandeis's closest companion on the Court, wrote in a letter to Harold Laski in 1921, "I am not sure that he [Brandeis] wouldn't burn me at a low fire if it were in the interest of some very possibly disinterested aim."[27] In all of this we have glimpses of the rigor of Brandeis's stance alone and apart from others.

But there was, at the same time, a contradictory pull in Brandeis in both his personal style and his intellectual commitments. Here was a man who spoke in 1890 of the need for "some retreat from the world, . . . [and for] solitude and privacy," who later espoused the "right to be let alone" as the "most comprehensive of rights and the right most valued by civilized men." And yet here was Brandeis writing in 1893 to a young associate in his law firm: "No hermit can be a great lawyer. . . . [S]uccess in advising others [comes] with the confidence which you yourself feel in your powers. That confidence can never come from books; it is gained by human intercourse."[28] Recall too that Brandeis purposefully turned away from the "retreat from the world" that can be found in an academic career to remain engaged not only in private law practice but in an extensive involvement in public affairs. And here was Brandeis as justice, in another notable dissent, proclaiming: "All rights are derived from the purposes of the society in which they exist; above all rights rises duty to the community."[29]

There was, then, a tension in Brandeis that can be seen in both his personal and his intellectual commitments—a tension between "solitude" and "human intercourse," between individualism and communal duty. But Brandeis did more than unwittingly represent these conflicting elements in Western liberal thought. He found a way of expressing and even exploiting their tension. He found a place to stand both in and apart from his society. He was neither insider nor outsider. He found a unique place for himself, poised always at the boundary.

This self-conscious marginality is discernible throughout his career; it was evident in his unconventional professional self-conception as judge of his clients and as the "people's lawyer." But in retrospect this conception was a rehearsal for Brandeis's fuller expression of his vocation. He found this expression both in Zionism and as a judge. Brandeis did not of course create either the Zionist movement or the United States Supreme Court. They were already well-established enterprises when he came to them. But he seized both as opportunities to act on a conception of himself both within and apart from his society and developed a conception both of Zionism and of the Court that differed markedly from his contemporaries' understanding of them.

His difference in perspective from other Zionists led ultimately to Brandeis's repudiation by, and resignation from, the movement in 1921, only one year after he had refused to accept the presidency of the World Zionist Organization.[30] In 1920 Brandeis explained his decision to refuse the presidency to the American delegation at the World Zionist Congress:

> I have become more and more convinced that, treated purely as a question of Zionism, it would be a mistake for me to resign from the Bench with a view to taking up definitely and exclusively this work. . . . I feel and have felt that if I retired from the Bench . . . all we have been saying is not true—that a man cannot be a Zionist and a good citizen of his country because there was Brandeis, who was supposed to be one of the most American of Americans who left his court and his country at the time that many will believe to be, its greatest need.[31]

Here too Brandeis thus portrayed himself as marginal, neither wholly in nor wholly outside Zionism, a self-conception that in itself gave offense to other Zionists. The very fact that Brandeis would not resign from the Supreme Court to assume the Zionist leadership was viewed as proof by many Zionists of his insufficient dedication to the cause.[32]

The eastern European Zionist leaders, and Chaim Weizmann in particular, were much more openly convinced of this proposition than their American counterparts.[33] For the American Jews, recently emigrated from eastern Europe, Brandeis's unwillingness to leave the Court mirrored their own desire to remain attached to America while working for a Jewish homeland in Palestine. But the American Zionists nonetheless took Weizmann's side in the dispute with Brandeis that openly erupted in 1921, and this was the occasion for Brandeis's abrupt resignation from the movement.

The specific dispute that was the occasion for Brandeis's resignation seems trivial now (the principal issue was whether donated and earned funds would be commingled or kept separate in Zionist accounts), and it was almost irrelevant even then, since the victorious Weizmann faction soon adopted all of the accounting and administrative proposals espoused by Brandeis and his defeated supporters. On its surface the split between Brandeis and Weizmann might appear little more than a dispute between western and eastern Europeans, with Brandeis's insistence on precise financial accounting and orderly administration the caricatured German to Weizmann's heedlessly passionate Russian. (One of Weizmann's allies even suggested that the true difference between him and Brandeis was that between Jew and gentile.)[34]

These issues were "camouflage," as the leading historian of American Zionism puts it.[35] The real issue was, as the Weizmann group saw, *Yiddishkeit*—wholeheartedness of feeling, a messianic, almost mystical identification with the Jewish people and its yearning for a home. It was here that Brandeis was found wanting and, in fact, held back.[36]

In its deepest import, the division between Brandeis and Weizmann came from their different responses to the shared underlying premise that drew both men to Zionism. This premise was succinctly put by Theodore Herzl, the modern founder of Zionism, when someone suggested to him that Palestine was needed only as a home for homeless Jews. Herzl responded, "All Jews have homes and yet they are all homeless."[37] This conviction, the emotional center of Zionism, was shared with equal fervor by both Weizmann and Brandeis. But Weizmann maintained that all Jews could find a home in Palestine.[38] Brandeis did not.

As much as Brandeis ever articulated his contrary belief, it was that Palestine should be available for all Jews, but that it was an appropriate home for some and not for others.[39] Brandeis never set out the differentiating criteria in general terms. He did, however, clearly conclude that Palestine would not be his home. This was one implication of his decision in 1920 to remain a justice of the United States Supreme Court. As I read Brandeis, his turning away from Palestine as a personal homeland was not from reluctance to yield the power or prestige of his judicial office; nor was it from a conviction that he had found a satisfactory home in America.

Indeed, Brandeis's attitude toward Palestine was significantly shaped by his dissatisfactions with American life—most notably by his conviction that large-scale economic and social organization, the "curse of bigness," threatened basic democratic values in America. The critical element for charting the future development of Palestine, according to Brandeis, was to ensure the dominance of self-supporting people mostly engaged in agricultural pursuits. Brandeis's vision for Palestine was, as he directly acknowledged, the embodiment of the Jeffersonian model of an independent farmer-yeomanry as the bulwark of democracy.[40]

Though Palestine would thus be an idealized version of American democracy, this did not imply for Brandeis that he or American Jews generally should emigrate to Palestine in order to realize the democratic ideals that could no longer be attained in America. Brandeis believed that Palestine, if organized on Jeffersonian principles, would serve as a beacon light for American democracy itself, recalling this country to its own best possibilities. This is what Brandeis meant when he said in 1914, "To be good Americans, we must be better Jews, and to be better Jews we must become Zionists."[41]

The only homeland that Brandeis wholeheartedly embraced was thus an imaginary place—not America as it was, but only a romanticized Jeffersonian vision of a past America, and not Palestine as it was, but this same romantic vision of a future Zion. These visions were not abstractions for Brandeis. He was passionately attached to them, as if driven by a wish to find a perfect homeland truly worthy of his unambivalent approval. His observation in a letter to his wife in 1919, during his first visit to Palestine, conveys this passion: "the ages-long longing—the love is all explicable now."[42] As he reported to his American Zionist followers after his return, on seeing Palestine itself, "you understand how the love and longing of the Jewish people have survived these eighteen hundred years."[43] Justice Holmes observed that, when Brandeis returned from this trip, he seemed "transfigured by his experience."[44]

In final analysis, however, Brandeis kept his distance from the possible realization of this passion. He confined his own "ages-long longing—the love" to a wholly imaginary object. Brandeis never admitted that his vision for transforming America according to the Jeffersonian blueprint was impractical though its unreality was clear at the time.[45] Palestine did hold some realistic possibility for development according to his professed ideals; but Brandeis held back from full personal commitment to Palestine in a way that ultimately led to his withdrawal from the Zionist movement. There were of course many different, practical reasons that led to Brandeis's withdrawal. At its heart, however, I see the same underlying premise that can be seen in all of Brandeis's endeavors—his conception of himself as always standing apart from others even though strongly attracted and attractive to them.

This, I believe, is the gripping force that Brandeis felt in Herzl's dictum that all Jews have homes but are homeless. Many Jews like Chaim Weizmann embraced Zionism hoping to end this paradoxical status, but Brandeis embraced the paradox. He came to Zionism by a route that most Zionists had not traveled. For most the syllogism was "I am a Jew and therefore homeless; I will find a home in Zion." For Brandeis the sequence was reversed. He knew he was homeless before he fully recognized his Jewishness; it is as if he concluded, "I am homeless and therefore a Jew; and this homeless Jewishness finds clearest expression in Zionism."

The attraction of Zionism for Brandeis was not its promise of an ultimate homeland. Zionism offered Brandeis an alternative to conceiving of himself as a fully assimilated American, as a person who had found a comfortable home here. Just as Brandeis had earlier held to the unconventional professional role as judge of, rather than reflexive advocate for, his clients, just as he virtually invented the role of public interest lawyer to maintain his independence from both corporate and popular clienteles, so he expressed this same vision of himself as a Zionist—as a man who stood apart from others, always turning away from any safe or comfortable resting place, always seeking, but never finding, an ideal home.

This vision was also at the heart of Brandeis's conception of his role as a judge. The Supreme Court was, of course, no more a blank canvas for Brandeis than Zionism. But it was also no less that; as with Zionism, there were aspects of the judicial institution that lent themselves readily to expression of Brandeis's vision of himself. Judges in our constitutional scheme—independent, life-tenured, black-robed—stand both in and apart from their society. Brandeis seized these characteristics and put them to the service of a more intense conception of social distance in the judicial role, of the judge standing at the boundary between social insiders and outsiders.

The conventional conception posits that a judge must stand apart from contending litigants in order to arrive at a disinterested, and thus fair, resolution of their dispute. But Brandeis pressed this conception of impartial distance a step further. His special vision emerges with greatest clarity in the most important recurrent issue that came before the Court during his tenure—the question of the proper judicial attitude toward economic and social regulatory legislation that cut into traditional prerogatives of property. Brandeis argued, most often in dissent, that the Court should not invalidate such legislation.

He and Oliver Wendell Holmes repeatedly came to this same conclusion, but each followed a very different route.[46] To pursue the spatial metaphor I have used for Brandeis, Holmes was more wholly removed, more detached from his society than Brandeis, who stood alone but always at the edge looking in.[47] Brandeis in this sense was less complacent than Holmes, more torn by wanting a home worthy of his wholehearted devotion, yet unable to find this home and unwilling to settle for less. Holmes by contrast had found a home for himself outside—as others have put it, outside and above, gazing skeptically down "as from Olympus."[48]

Brandeis's difference in perspective from Holmes never emerged sharply in his judicial opinions, but in less formal settings it was unmistakable. Dean Acheson recounted an episode when a mistaken (implicit) concordance with Holmes was forcefully corrected:

> [Brandeis's] severity in his analysis of fact, in reducing the issue involved to the minimum possible [in his opinions] . . . misled many of his admirers about his basic nature. I remember one evening during the twenties listening to Professor Manley Hudson of Harvard . . . hold forth on Brandeis, the Scientist of the Law, who had brought the methods of the laboratory into the courthouse, who put facts through test-tube treatment, and so on. While this was going on, I found out that the Justice was free and would receive my friend and me. It was easy to guide the conversation to the growing political issue of prohibition and, in the course of it, to provoke Mr. Hudson into asserting that moral principles were no more than generalizations from the mores or accepted notions of a particular time and place.
>
> The eruption was even more spectacular than I had

> anticipated. The Justice wrapped the mantle of Isaiah around himself, dropped his voice a full octave, jutted his eyebrows forward in a most menacing way, and began to prophesy. Morality was truth; and truth had been revealed to man in an unbroken, continuous, and consistent flow by the great prophets and poets of all time. He quoted Goethe in German and from Euripides via Gilbert Murray. On it went—an impressive, almost frightening, glimpse of an elemental force.
>
> When, at length, we were on the sidewalk [outside Brandeis's home], I asked Hudson what he thought now about the Scientist of the Law. He stood there shaking with emotion. . . . "Monstrous!" he kept saying. "It's monstrous!" Here, indeed, was proof of my thesis expounded to Felix Frankfurter [in his 1920 letter, while Brandeis's clerk], "that if some of his [Brandeis's] admirers knew him better they would like him less."[49]

Brandeis's moralism took a different form in his judicial opinions. But it was there and pervasive, even in his dissenting opinions in agreement with (and often joined by) Holmes, arguing against the Court's invalidation of some legislative enactment. In these dissents it was never enough for Brandeis (though it was essentially enough for Holmes) that a popular majority had formally approved the challenged legislation.[50] Brandeis always demanded something more, though he never fully articulated what that more was.

The current conventional account of Brandeis's jurisprudence tends to obscure his difference with Holmes (perhaps because Brandeis never clearly formulated it himself) and to yoke the two men (together with Frankfurter) as charter members of the Harvard school of reflexive judicial deference to majoritarian institutions.[51] Holmes was not thus misled, however; he saw that Brandeis's conception of the judicial role significantly differed from his. Holmes noted the difference, though he did not adequately understand it, in a 1930 letter to

Harold Laski: "I told [Brandeis] long ago that he really was an advocate rather than a Judge. He is affected by his interest in a cause, and if he feels it he is not detached."[52] Frankfurter made a similar, though more delicately phrased, observation in a published tribute to Brandeis in 1932: "Of course, a life-long study of history and deep immersion in affairs have bent him to certain preferences. And since cases are not just cases, but imply alternative social policies, his predilections may decide cases."[53]

The fact that these accusations of insufficient "detachment," of judicial "predilections" rather than "neutrality,"[54] came from Holmes and Frankfurter should alert us to the possibility that Brandeis did not truly qualify for membership in the Harvard school. To adapt Dean Acheson's observation, those who knew him best embraced him least. It is not true, however, that Brandeis simply hid his social policy preferences behind his constitutional adjudications; there was a more subtle advocacy than this in his jurisprudence, and its very subtlety has made the differentiation that Holmes and Frankfurter saw at the time less visible to latter-day viewers.

One way to grasp the distinctive element of his jurisprudence is simply to note the length of his opinions compared with Holmes's (or indeed with those written by most of his contemporary colleagues). Brandeis's opinions were so long because they were filled with extensive consideration of the reasons why the legislature had enacted the measures under review and the justifiability of those reasons. His opinions thus read like advocacy of the merits of the legislation. For example, Justice Harlan Fiske Stone wrote to Brandeis about his dissenting opinion to uphold a state statute imposing tax burdens on chain stores and favoring individual enterprises: "I think you are too much an advocate of this particular legislation. I have little enthusiasm for it, although I think it constitutional. In any case I think our dissents are more effective if we take the attitude that we are concerned with power and not with the merits of its exercise."[55] For Brandeis, however, the question of constitutional "power" to enact legislation and the "merits" of legislation could not so readily be separated.

Brandeis explained his rationale for his lengthy opinions and seeming advocacy of the legislative merits in his 1924 dissent in *Jay Burns Baking Company v. Bryan*.[56] The Nebraska legislature had required that all bread be sold to ultimate consumers at a standard weight. The Court, in an opinion by Justice Pierce Butler, invalidated the law on the grounds that it "was not necessary for the protection of consumers" and thus violated the Fourteenth Amendment.[57] Brandeis's dissent (joined by Holmes) occupies seventeen pages in the United States Reports; fifteen and one-half pages are wholly devoted to factual recitation of the history and purposes of bread weight regulations in the United States from 1858 onward (and on thirteen of these pages the footnotes fill at least half of the printed space). At the very end of his dissent, Brandeis explained his purpose in setting out this extended factual account:

> Much evidence referred to by me is not in the record. Nor could it have been included. It is the history of the experience gained under similar legislation, and the result of scientific experiments made, since the entry of the judgment below [invalidating the state act]. Of such events in our history, whether occurring before or after the enactment of the statute or the entry of the judgment, the Court should acquire knowledge and must, in my opinion, take judicial notice, whenever required to perform the delicate judicial task here involved. . . . Put at its highest, our function is to determine, in the light of all facts which may enrich our knowledge and enlarge our understanding, whether the measure . . . transcends the bounds of reason. That is, whether the provision as applied is so clearly arbitrary or capricious that legislators acting reasonably could not have believed it to be necessary or appropriate for the public welfare.[58]

In the final half-sentence Brandeis tied his enterprise into the conventional doctrinal formula, which evolved in later judicial uses into the articulated standard for so-called "deferential" review of legislative rationality under the equal protection clause.[59] His invocation of this formula makes it easy to misread him as a matriculant of the Harvard school. But his true purpose, as well as the premise that ordinarily led him to defer to legislative enactments, was more accurately expressed in the penultimate observation quoted above, that the judicial function, as he saw it, was "to determine . . . whether the measure . . . transcends the bounds of reason." Brandeis did not mean by this "rationality" in its more recent judicial sense. I believe he meant "the bounds of reason" as fair-minded, tolerant men (as he saw them) would define reason. This was not "rationality" but "reasonableness." Brandeis had a wider conception of "reasonableness" than the majority of his brethren; but he shared with them, and differed with Holmes, in his insistence that majoritarian legislation generally must submit to some extrinsic criterion.

Brandeis's conception of "reasonableness" and of his judicial role in this determination were in effect the same conception of substance and role that he had held in his earlier work as a private mediator in disputes between capital and labor. There is a direct concordance between his observation in the *Jay Burns Baking Company* case and his address in 1904 to an employers' group setting out the principles that would lead to "industrial peace and prosperity":

> Employers and employees should try to agree. . . . Nine-tenths of the serious controversies which arise in life result from misunderstanding, result from one man not knowing the facts which to the other man seem important, or otherwise failing to appreciate his point of view. A properly conducted conference [to resolve labor disputes] involves a frank disclosure of such facts—patient, careful argument, willingness to listen and to consider.[60]

Brandeis amplified these views in a letter he wrote in 1910, following his mediation of a New York garment workers' strike (his first extensive contact with eastern European Jewish immigrants):

> What struck me most was that each side had a great capacity for placing themselves in the other fellows' shoes. There was the usual bitterness and rancor but despite this, each side was willing to admit the reality of the other fellows' predicament. They really understood each other, and admitted the understanding. They argued but they were willing to listen to argument. That set these people apart in my experience in labor disputes.[61]

Brandeis drew his notion of the proper judicial role from this conception. The judge should not only be "willing . . . to listen and to consider"; he should visibly display this willingness so that the disputants themselves would follow the judge's example in their own future dealings and would be led by the judge to understand one another's perspectives. By this conception, there is no special judicial methodology of legal reasoning distinct from "politics" or "policy considerations." There is only one method of reasoning, the proper method in a democratic polity: the method of "reasonableness," which the judge above all should exemplify.[62]

Brandeis's persistent campaign against large-scale social and economic enterprise—the "curse of bigness," as he called it[63]—was intimately connected to his conviction that all citizens in a democracy (and not merely judges) are obliged to engage in self-justifying "patient, careful argument," and that "peace and prosperity" will most likely arise from "willingness to listen and to consider." Brandeis relied on this principle in his judicial capacity when he voted to strike down several important New Deal measures in 1935.[64]

The most notable of these decisions was the *Schecter Poultry Company* case, in which the Court invalidated the National

Recovery Act, holding that Congress had failed to provide any legislative standards to control its administration and had asserted authority over transactions falling exclusively within state authority to regulate commerce. Brandeis did not write in this case, though he joined the Court's opinion. He vividly explained his own version of the Court's holding, however, in a conversation with Thomas Corcoran (a member of President Roosevelt's "brain trust") in the justices' robing room immediately after the decision had been announced. According to Corcoran, Brandeis appeared "visibly excited and deeply agitated" and said to him: "This is the end of this business of centralization, and I want you to go back and tell the President that we're not going to let this government centralize everything. It's come to an end. As for your young men . . . tell them to go home, back to the States. That is where they must do their work."[65]

This ex cathedra pronouncement can readily be translated into terms of Brandeis's criterion of "reasonableness" for evaluating the constitutionality of legislation. The central flaw of the NRA was not, for him, its substantive provisions; the flaw was that it was not enacted by a publicly visible or accessible process of reasoning. That Congress, rather than the states, had acted, and that Congress had delegated regulatory authority wholesale, without clear guiding standards, to NRA administrators meant for Brandeis that "patient, careful argument" and visibly detailed consideration of conflicting perspectives among disputants had not occurred in the enactment of the legislation and would not reliably take place in its implementation. The NRA was essentially opaque to reasoned discourse and, in this sense, was unreasonable.

Since Holmes had left the Court by 1935, Brandeis's position in these New Deal cases does not mark a clear-cut difference with him.[66] Brandeis's underlying concern in these cases and Holmes's indifference to this concern were, however, repeatedly (though only implicitly) contrasted in their work as justices. In the very extensiveness of his opinions, Brandeis demonstrated that he seriously accepted the obligation to explain and justify. Holmes's compressed, epigrammatic style of opinion-writing was the antithesis of Brandeis's, and it carried the opposite implication. Just as Holmes espoused deference to majoritarian institutions because of their hierarchically superior "democratic" authority rather than because of the demonstrated reasonableness of their measures, he was also prepared to assert in his swift and conclusory opinions that judicial authority was self-validating rather than obligated to provide reasoned justification.[67]

The simple fact that Brandeis and Holmes almost invariably voted together to uphold the constitutionality of economic and social legislation should thus not obscure the critical differences in their perspectives. It is also relevant that most of the laws challenged during their joint tenure on the Court were measures restricting corporate enterprise. Brandeis clearly favored such "social experiments" in ways diametrically opposed to Holmes.[68] This does not in itself mean that Brandeis was dispositively moved by these sympathies; it does mean that Holmes, more than Brandeis, was forced to set aside his distaste for such legislation when he voted to uphold it.[69] If (as Frankfurter later appeared to maintain) this form of self-flagellation is the critical test of a suitably detached judicial temperament, then Brandeis was never as much an initiate as Holmes.

There was one notable occasion when the basic disagreement between Brandeis and Holmes was more sharply etched than usual. This was the Court's 1923 decision in *Meyer v. Nebraska*.[70] Justice James McReynolds wrote the Court's opinion holding that a state law forbidding German language instruction to elementary school children violated constitutionally protected "liberty."[71] Though Brandeis and Holmes usually dissented together from the Court majority's regular invocation of "liberty" to overturn state laws, this time Brandeis joined the Court's opinion while Holmes dissented. The state law, Holmes argued, "might . . . be regarded as a reasonable or even necessary method" of ensuring that all citizens "should speak a common tongue"; and "if it is reasonable, [the law] is not an undue restriction of . . . liberty."[72] Holmes concluded his dissent with an observation apparently borrowed from Brandeis's usual vocabulary: "I am unable to say," Holmes said, "that the Constitution of the United States prevents the experiment being tried."[73]

Brandeis silently joined the Court's opinion and thus did not explain the distinction he saw between this particular state "experiment" and others that passed constitutional muster for him. The following summer, however, Brandeis discussed this case with Felix Frankfurter; according to Frankfurter's somewhat garbled notes of that conversation, Brandeis generally opposed any use of "liberty" as a substantive limit on state legislation and preferred to restrict the Fourteenth Amendment guarantee to "procedural regularity." So long as the Court majority generally employed a substantive conception of constitutional liberty, however, Brandeis concluded that this conception should not be restricted to property regulations, but should extend to matters such as the "right to your education [and] to utter speech." Holmes by contrast, according to Brandeis, did not want to extend the substantive scope of the Fourteenth Amendment in any way.[74]

From Frankfurter's account of their conversation, it appears that Brandeis would have preferred to abandon his position in *Meyer* if only the Court majority repudiated their willingness to strike down other kinds of state laws as infringements on "liberty." Notwithstanding Brandeis's protestations to Frankfurter, however, I believe that logical consistency with then-prevalent constitutional doctrine was not the basic reason for Brandeis's vote to overturn the state law in *Meyer.* I believe that he was more fundamentally moved by the specific context of the state law—that it was obviously enacted as a derogation of the German-speaking minority in Nebraska in direct response to the passions unleashed by the war against Germany. Brandeis may have been specifically affected by the personal identifications provoked by this law, since his family had conversed at home in German and his own elementary education had been conducted in a German-speaking school in Louisville.[75] Whatever the role of this specific personal involvement, I believe more fundamentally that Brandeis's vote in *Meyer* came from his instinctive sympathy with oppressed outsiders—an impulse that was not enlisted from Brandeis on behalf of the capitalists who regularly succeeded in persuading a majority of the Court to protect their "fundamental liberty" from economic regulations favoring laborers or consumers.

Holmes did not distinguish between the "liberty" claimed by capitalists and by the German-speaking minority; neither, so far as he was concerned, deserved constitutional protection against majority rule.[76] He did not share Brandeis's instinctive sympathy for outsiders. This was the basic difference in their conceptions of themselves as judges. Their disagreement in *Meyer* was the most overt judicial expression of this difference (though even here, of course, it was masked by Brandeis's silent concurrence in the Court's opinion).[77]

The openness of Brandeis's advocacy of "Progressive" legislation in his judicial opinions, criticized as such by Holmes, was another (though also muted) indication of this difference between the two men and of Brandeis's instinctive sympathy for outsiders. Brandeis understood that when conventional judges reviewed the constitutionality of economic regulatory legislation, they could not begin to comprehend how a "reasonable case" could be made for the laws. These judges were so deeply embued with the pieties and prejudices of their comfortable life experience and status that they could not even glimpse the legislation from the perspective of its adherents; they could not readily "admit the reality of the other fellows' predicament." Thus Brandeis saw himself obliged to illuminate, to emphasize, to advocate this "other fellows'" point of view in order, as he put it in his *Jay Burns Baking Company* dissent, to "enrich [his brethren's] knowledge and enlarge [their] understanding" of that point of view.[78] As Holmes clearly saw, however, this was not a "detached" exercise for Brandeis; his passions were engaged. He spoke for these "other fellows," these excluded outsiders, because he sensed a special kinship with them.

Perhaps the clearest instance of this passionate espousal of the outsider's perspective in Brandeis's judicial writings appeared in a dissenting opinion that he never published because he was ultimately able to persuade his brethren to approve the result he sought. I cite this unpublished opinion at some length because Brandeis revealed a passion and a biting anger on behalf of the disfavored outsiders in that case that was invariably more muted in his published opinions, even in his dissents. I suspect that if this opinion had ever been published, Brandeis would have damped down these elements, both from his innate reticence regarding public revelations of deep feeling and his equal reluctance to inflict irrevocable wounds on adversaries.[79] But neither constraint had yet been fully imposed on Brandeis's draft dissent in the *Coronado Coal Company* case, which he wrote in 1921–22.[80]

The case arose in the wake of a violent struggle between one coal company and the mineworkers union. Brandeis evoked this struggle in an almost novelistic passage at the beginning of his opinion:

> In the mountains of western Arkansas, near the village of Frogtown, were nine small coal mines which Bache and Denman managed as a business unit. Arkansas was "organized territory." That is, all the mines there were operated as union shops under agreement with the United Mine Workers of America. [citation omitted] The Bache-Denman mines had been so operated since

> 1903, when the first of them was opened. In 1913 (or before) the business became unprofitable. Bache and Denman were led to believe that this was due to union exactions and restrictions. The superintendent proposed operation on the open shop basis; but he advised that the change would involve "a bitter fight" and that "the success of this plan means the utter annihilation of the union so far as our mines are concerned."[81]

Brandeis then recounted how Bache and Denman acted on the superintendent's proposal and how apt his prediction had been:

> The mine was shut down and all employees were discharged. Soon guards arrived, men furnished by a private detective agency, experienced and well supplied with rifles and ammunition. All removable inflammable material around the mine was taken away. A wire rope was stretched around the enclosure. Notices were posted warning all but employees off the premises. Electric lights were placed at intervals with reflectors throwing the light outside of the enclosure. As soon as the entrenchment had been completed, non-union men, from neighboring States, were brought in at intervals, in small numbers. On Saturday, April 4, 1914, operations at the mine were resumed but as an "open shop."[82]

Brandeis swiftly related the escalating events between 4 April and 17 July, when "armed men, undoubtedly unionists" killed several mine employees and guards and then destroyed the mine and surrounding property by fire and dynamiting. He then turned to an evaluation of the relative legal and moral claims of the antagonists, which I cite at some length:

> Throughout these trying months the operators acted strictly within their legal rights. The unionists, on the other hand, had been lawless aggressors. . . . No fact

urged by them in extenuation would, if established, afford legal justification for any of the injury inflicted. . . . The unionists say . . . that the operators were determined to lower their standard of living by destroying their union and forcing a reduction of wages, longer hours of work and more burdensome working conditions; and that the guards had insulted women and children, had procured illegal arrests of unionists and had generally terrorized the community. Obviously such acts, no matter how aggravated, would afford no excuse in law for malicious destruction of plaintiffs' business and mining properties. Nor is there any basis for a claim that the destruction was wrought in the exercise of any right of self-defense recognized by the law.

To destroy a business is illegal. It is not illegal to lower the standard of working men's living or to destroy the union which aims to raise or maintain such a standard. A business is property; the law protects it; and a statute which denies to its owner the right to protection by injunction against striking employees violates the Fourteenth Amendment, although there is no threat of violence or of injury to tangible property. *Truax v. Corrigan,* decided December 19, 1921. A man's standard of living is not property; and the law does not protect it by injunction or otherwise. Statutes designed to maintain or raise the workingman's standard of living, by affording labor unions protection against employers discriminating against union members, are unconstitutional. *Adair v. United States,* 208 U.S. 161 [1908]; *Coppage v. Kansas,* 236 U.S. 1 [1915]. Even the right to self-help by means of a strike against such discrimination has been denied to the unions in some jurisdictions. And, although the employment be at will, persons may not be solicited to join the union while so employed, if they have agreed as a condition of employment not to join the union. *Hitchman Coal & Coke Co. v. Mitchell* [245 U.S. 229 (1917)]. Nor may a union protect itself by a refusal of its members to work upon the product of an employer

> who is attacking the union, if the necessary effect of such refusal is to injure a third person. *Duplex Printing Co. v. Deering,* 254 U.S. 443 [1921]. Such being the law every citizen should obey it; and the court must enforce it. It may be morally wrong to use legal processes, great financial resources and a high intelligence to lower miners' standards of living; but so long as the law sanctions it, economic force may not be repelled by physical force. If union members deem the law unwise or unjust, they may, like other American citizens, exercise their political right to change it by new legislation, and, if need be, by constitutional amendment.[83]

Brandeis then moved to his specific legal argument—that no matter how clearly the unionists' actions violated Arkansas or federal laws, in the case at hand they had been sued by the mine operators for violating the Sherman Anti-Trust Act by allegedly conspiring to interfere with interstate commerce; and coal mining was not "interstate commerce" as defined by the prevailing Supreme Court doctrine in related contexts. The Court majority had rejected Brandeis's view in conference. But before the decision was rendered, Chief Justice Edward Douglass White died and was replaced by former President William Howard Taft; the case was reargued, and Taft was ultimately persuaded to write a position adopting Brandeis's position, which became the unanimous opinion of the Court.[84] Brandeis filed his dissent away. In a later conversation about the case with Felix Frankfurter, he observed: "They will take it from Taft but wouldn't take it from me. If it is good enough for Taft, it is good enough for us, they say—and a natural sentiment."[85]

Taft's opinion for the Court contained none of the biting irony of Brandeis's draft dissent, no juxtaposing of the law's protection of the property of employers and employees in their livelihoods, no suggestion of the moral wrong involved in massing the law, money, and "high intelligence to lower miners' standards of living." But Taft was an insider; Brandeis was not. Indeed, Taft was one of the grandees of the American bar who had publicly opposed Brandeis's confirmation to the Court.[86] Though the relationship between Brandeis and Taft on the Court became, by all accounts, quite cordial,[87] Brandeis's remark to Frankfurter (his closest confidant about Court matters during his tenure) suggests that even among his brethren Brandeis continued to see himself, and to be seen as, an outsider.

From his outsider's perspective Brandeis appreciated the frustration and anger of the union men in ways that his more comfortable and complacent colleagues could not comprehend. In 1919, just two years before the Court first heard the *Coronado* case, Brandeis had written his wife, "Old Boston is unregenerate and I am not sorry to have escaped [by his Court appointment] a struggle there as nasty as it is unending."[88] In the midst of his confirmation battle in 1916, Brandeis had written to his brother: "At all events the country including Boston will know what I have been 'up against.' I suppose eighteen centuries of Jewish persecution must have enured me to such hardships and developed the like of a duck's back."[89]

If Brandeis did not explicitly invoke the sources of his affinity with the oppressed miners in his *Coronado* dissent, the empathy was there nonetheless; though more muted in expression, this attitude was also at work in his published opinions addressing the constitutionality of social and economic regulatory legislation. This sympathetic identification with one of the adversaries in the disputes between capital and labor was, I believe, the basis for Holmes's charge, in his letter to Laski, that Brandeis "really was an advocate rather than a Judge . . . affected by his interest in a cause, and if he feels it he is not detached."

There is some irony in this criticism of Brandeis as a judge, that he was too much the advocate, in light of the earlier critique by those opposed to his confirmation that as an attorney he was too much the judge. But there is a deeper unity in these two seemingly different stances by Brandeis. In both settings he strove for detached, impartial judgment. But in the disputes pitting capital against labor that came to his Supreme Court, Brandeis maintained that impartial resolution was not possible unless a judge could "appreciate [the] point of view" of both sides. This was Brandeis's charge to employers when he served as a labor mediator, and this was his prescription to his colleagues on the bench. This was the aim, as I have suggested, of his extended compilation of the facts in each case.

These facts were not dry data for Brandeis; they were suffused with the passion of the controversy, with the sense of oppression and frustrated rage of the workers or the consumers battling the great corporate forces of the day. Brandeis felt this and understood how these feelings could erupt into violence. These are the feelings that Brandeis personally invested in Zionism—his identification with the oppression and suppressed rage of homeless Jews and their longing for a true homeland.

To say that Brandeis instinctively understood and identified with these oppressed outsiders is not, however, to say that he saw himself as one of them. Brandeis was their advocate on the bench, as he had previously been their attorney, the "people's lawyer." In both places, as he had said in 1905, Brandeis insisted on "holding a position of independence, between the wealthy and the people, prepared to curb the excesses of either." Brandeis kept this independence, moreover, not only in the conflicts between rich and poor, but wherever he saw struggle between comfortable insider and scorned outsider. In these conflicts, Brandeis sought to occupy a middle ground between the disputants, between the insiders and outsiders.

In one sense, this middle ground was for Brandeis the place a mediator should seek, a common ground between the disputants that, when found, would serve as a basis for agreement. Thus the dispute would be resolved and, in this specific context, the insider/outsider distinction dissolved in favor of an inclusive communal identity among the previously opposed parties. In another and deeper sense, however, this independent middle ground served for Brandeis as an expression of his own rigorous solitude, his stance apart from others. Throughout his career, Brandeis remained at the social boundary between insider and outsider. He never conceived of himself as an insider, notwithstanding his early professional success and personal wealth or his later high judicial office. At the same time Brandeis was obviously separated from oppressed outsiders by his wealth and status. In this sense, then, he was neither insider nor outsider, but occupied a singular social space between the two.

Some have argued that Brandeis eagerly sought insider status at various times in his career, but that it was withheld from him because of anti-Semitism.[90] These scholars conclude that Brandeis's ostentatious advocacy on behalf of outsiders as the "people's lawyer" and as head of the American Zionist movement was a reaction to his own resentment at exclusion from Boston Brahminism. Even if the anti-Semitism Brandeis personally encountered was as sustained and as wounding to his self-esteem as these scholars maintain—and I share others' skepticism about these claims[91]—I find it difficult to believe that the extraordinary energy that Brandeis invested in his advocacy for outsiders before joining the Court, and the persistence of his stance on the Court, can be simply or even principally explained as an expression of Brandeis's resentment and thwarted social ambition.[92]

In the last chapter of this book, I shall offer some speculation about sources of Brandeis's identification with outsiders in his early familial experience unrelated to issues of Jewishness or anti-Semitism. At the moment, however, it is not necessary to resolve the question of Brandeis's motivations or their origins. The important point here is to see the distinctive role that Brandeis forged for himself, whatever its origins—

his socially marginal stance, his conception of himself as neither insider nor outsider but as occupying the boundary between these statuses, speaking as advocate for the outsider and working to dissolve the boundary. Brandeis seized on his own Jewishness, through the Zionist movement, as one expression of this social role. Jewishness can, however, find expression in a markedly different conception of social role. Brandeis's self-conscious marginality is not the only social role conceivable for an American Jew or for a Jewish justice on the United States Supreme Court.

3

Frankfurter

The two men were alike in many ways. Both held the same public office, of course; their terms even briefly overlapped: Frankfurter joined the Court on January 30 and Brandeis resigned on February 13, 1939. Both were Jews who had been educated at the Harvard Law School. And they were close friends for some twenty-five years. Indeed, though Frankfurter had a wide circle (his wife once observed that "Felix has two hundred best friends"),[1] for Brandeis their friendship was apparently the most intimate male relationship in his adult life. Most uncharacteristically, Brandeis referred to Frankfurter, in a letter to him in 1925, as "half brother–half son."[2]

Their differences were, however, substantial and are more significant in understanding the two men. There was first of all a difference in personal style. Compare Brandeis's guarded reserve, his apparent aloofness, with this description of Frankfurter:

> He talked copiously, with an overflowing gaiety and spontaneity which conveyed the impression of great natural sweetness. . . . Whenever I met him . . . the same phenomenon was always to be observed: he was the centre, the life and soul of a circle of eager and delighted human beings, exuberant, endlessly appreciative, delighting in every manifestation of intelligence, imagination or life.[3]

This was Isaiah Berlin's testimony of Frankfurter's visiting year at Oxford in 1934. Or compare the account by Brandeis's biographer of his clients' efforts to remain in his company "by clinging to some substantial object"[4] with Marion Frankfurter's description of her husband as a "door-hanger" who could not let a guest leave their home without "adding another paragraph."[5] Or compare the physical distance Brandeis kept between himself and his law clerks with Frankfurter's "habit" of taking other men's arms and "squeezing," as reported by one of his law clerks, among others.[6] (As one of Frankfurter's eulogizers put it after his death, "Who of us will not continue to feel that iron grip on the arm?")[7] Indeed, the best explanation of Brandeis's intimacy with Frankfurter is suggested by Isaiah Berlin's general observation that Frankfurter "had an uncommon capacity for melting reserve, breaking through inhibitions, and generally emancipating those with whom he came into contact."[8]

There were also substantial differences in their experience as Jews. By the time Frankfurter reached the Harvard Law School as a student in 1903 (and even more when he joined its faculty in 1914), Jewishness had assumed an openly stigmatized meaning in American life. The two men's Jewishness also had very different meanings in personal terms. Unlike Brandeis, Frankfurter was raised as a practicing Jew. "As a boy," he recounted, "I was religiously observant. I wouldn't eat breakfast until I had done the religious devotions in the morning." Jewish ritual, he said, later "ceased to have inner meaning" for him; he first fully recognized this at a Yom Kippur service during his junior year at the City College of New York and thereupon "left the service in the middle of it, never to return."[9]

Frankfurter never denied that he was a Jew; he was quite pointed throughout his life in identifying himself as such. But there was no spiritual or "inner meaning" to this affiliation for him, whereas Brandeis, who never had any childhood involvement to abandon, did imbue his latter-day Zionism with a spiritual fervor. (Frankfurter also became active in Zionist affairs around World War I, but only as an aide-de-camp to Brandeis; after Brandeis's death in 1941, Frankfurter showed no special interest in the movement.)[10]

Jewishness also had different cultural meaning for the two men. Brandeis believed that his religious affiliation (which he equated with his Zionism) was wholly consistent with his Americanism. Frankfurter did not fully believe this; his early experience, in particular, taught him otherwise. For Frankfurter, Jewishness was inextricably linked to the immigrant world in which he had been raised. Brandeis was born here; Frankfurter arrived, when he was twelve, with his parents from Vienna. The family lived on the East Side of New York in the midst of a German-Jewish immigrant settlement.[11] Frankfurter recounted that when he arrived in New York, he "never had heard a word of English spoken"; he counted among the "greatest benefactors" in his life his first public school teacher, a "middle-aged Irish woman":

> She believed in corporal punishment—I was going to say capital punishment. She evidently saw this ardent kid who by that time had picked up some English—I'm not a linguist and haven't got a good ear for languages—but she told the boys that if anybody was caught speaking German with me, she would punish him. She would give gentle uppercuts to the boys. It was wonderful for me that speaking English was enforced upon my environment in school, all thanks to Miss Hogan.[12]

To become a full-fledged American, then, Frankfurter had to separate himself from his immigrant past—as it were, by force majeure, by corporal, if not capital, punishment. Frankfurter's boyhood Jewishness, like that of many other Jewish immigrants, was bound up in this struggle.[13]

All of these differences found expression in the underlying attitudes of the two men to American society. Brandeis, as I have suggested, always stood apart; he was content, even eager, to remain at the margin—in effect, homeless. This was not Felix Frankfurter's way. Early in his career, Frankfurter alluded to this issue in a letter to his mentor, Henry Stimson, explaining his regret that he could not affiliate with any political party: "I have to be one of those who, by being outside of both camps, is going to pick and choose from election to election. . . . I don't like the situation. It is not comfortable to be politically homeless, but I don't see my way clear to being other than a tenant at will until better days."[14]

Happier days did come later for Frankfurter when he embraced a political affiliation with a passion that many reserve for other pursuits. Two days before his death, Frankfurter told his chosen biographer, "Tell the whole story. Let people see how much I loved Roosevelt, how much I loved my country, and let them see how great a man Roosevelt really was."[15] Franklin Roosevelt was not the sole object of Frankfurter's adulation. At different times he spoke in similar terms of other national institutions—of the Supreme Court, on which he served ("Of all earthly institutions this Court comes nearest to having, for me, sacred aspects");[16] of Harvard, where he studied and taught ("I have a quasi-religious feeling about the Harvard Law School");[17] and about America itself.

In 1942 Frankfurter said this at a case conference with his brethren (as he later recorded in his diary):

> I am saying what I am going to say because perhaps this case arouses in me feelings that could not be entertained by anyone else around this table. It is well known that a convert is more zealous than one born to the faith. None of you has had the experience that I have had with reference to American citizenship. . . . As one who has no ties with any formal religion, perhaps the feelings that underlie religious forms for me run into intensification of my feelings about American citizenship. I have known, as you hardly could have known, literally hun-

> dreds of men and women of the finest spirit who had to shed old loyalties and take on the loyalty of American citizenship. Perhaps I can best convey what is in my mind if I read to you from a letter written by as distinguished an historian as is now alive when he went through this experience of becoming an American citizen.

Frankfurter then recited to his brethren, and transcribed in his diary, a letter from Professor Gaetano Salvemini of Harvard:

> There is in this country a wider area of generosity than in any other country,—at least in Europe. It is this feeling that one is at home here that conquers you little by little. And one fine day you feel that you are no longer an exile but a citizen in your own country. When I took my oath I felt that really I was performing a grand function. I was throwing away not my intellectual and moral but my juristic past. I threw it away without any regret.[18]

Frankfurter thus, according to his testimony, embraced American citizenship with an almost religious fervor, so that, like his correspondent, he was "no longer an exile" but "at home." The context in which Frankfurter gave this testimony suggests how this embrace found expression in his conception of the judicial role. The context was the Court's consideration of *Schneiderman v. United States,*[19] a case in which the government sought to revoke the petitioner's naturalized citizenship on the grounds that he was an active Communist party member when naturalized and that such membership in itself was necessarily inconsistent with his required oath of attachment "to the principles" of the Constitution. (The naturalization statute in effect at the time did not specify Communist party membership as a disqualification, and Schneiderman had neither revealed nor denied his membership then.)

Frankfurter voted for revocation in the case, though he wrote no opinion. From his diary entry, I would paraphrase his underlying attitude as follows: I, like Schneiderman, was once an alien; unlike him I "shed old loyalties," and he must do the same; I say this not as a private individual but as a judge charged with defining what it means to be an American, to be truly welcome and "at home" here. Frankfurter, in my paraphrase, portrays himself as a quintessential insider—even as a "convert . . . more zealous than one born to the faith."

This self-portrayal found more open, and even more dramatic, expression in a case that had come to the Court two years earlier, *Minersville School District v. Gobitis*.[20] The school board required all children to salute and recite allegiance to the American flag at the beginning of each school day. Jehovah's Witness children refused on the grounds that this was idolatry forbidden by their religion; they were accordingly expelled, and their parents were convicted of truancy law violations for effectively withholding them from school attendance. Frankfurter wrote the Court's opinion affirming the school board's authority to compel the flag salute.

Chief Justice Charles Evans Hughes recounted that he had assigned the opinion to Frankfurter because of the emotion with which Frankfurter had invoked, in the conference deliberation, the "role of the public school in instilling love of country," based on his own experience as an immigrant child.[21] As Richard Danzig has observed, Frankfurter's *Gobitis* opinion echoes his reminiscences of one of his "greatest benefactors," Miss Hogan, who forced Frankfurter to speak only English by threatening "gentle uppercuts," if not "capital punishment," to anyone conversing in an alien tongue with him.[22]

This resonance is only indirect. In his opinion Frankfurter carefully confined himself to the proposition only that a reasonable legislature might favor compulsory observances to "best promote in the minds of children . . . an attachment to the institutions of their country," to "evoke in them appreciation of the nation's hopes and dreams, its sufferings and sacrifices," and that a court must defer to such reasonable legislative judgment.[23] It may be that the local school board were thus benignly motivated in expelling the Jehovah's Witness children and prosecuting their parents. It may also be that the board were more intent on expressing disdain for these stiff-necked aliens in their midst who refused to acknowledge the supremacy of their secular authority. Even this less appealing state policy found some implicit deference in Frankfurter's opinion. The Jehovah's Witnesses, he suggested, were "dissidents" asking for "exceptional immunity";[24] the question at issue was the "respect" required for their "individual idiosyncracies."[25] In a gentle uppercut of his own devising, he wrote: "For ourselves, we might be tempted to say that the deepest patriotism is best engendered by giving unfettered scope to the most crochety beliefs. . . . But the courtroom is not the arena for debating issues of educational policy."[26]

Thus Frankfurter was prepared to assume the most benign legislative motive, but even to accept a more disdainful hostility to alien beliefs and practices, in order to vindicate "authority to safeguard the nation's fellowship" by imposing "the binding tie of cohesive sentiment" toward the symbols of the nation.[27] His is the voice of the insider—unsympathetic, uncomprehending, dismissive of the outsider's "idiosyncracies," his "crochety beliefs." This is a far remove from Brandeis's habitual stance of trying "to appreciate [the other man's] point of view" and his persistent effort in judicial opinions to set out the most sympathetic case for others' perspectives in order "to enrich our knowledge and enlarge our understanding" of them.[28]

Frankfurter carried all but one of his brethren with him in *Gobitis;* only Harlan Fiske Stone dissented. Just three years later, however, in one of the most abrupt reversals in its history, the Court overturned *Gobitis*. Frankfurter dissented, while three justices—Hugo Black, William O. Douglas, and Frank Murphy—who had previously voted with him in *Gobitis* now reversed themselves to form the new Court majority (with Stone and two new arrivals, Robert Jackson and Wiley

Rutledge). These were the opening words of Frankfurter's dissent:

> One who belongs to the most vilified and persecuted minority in history is not likely to be insensible to the freedoms guaranteed by our Constitution. Were my purely personal attitude relevant I should wholeheartedly associate myself with the general libertarian views in the Court's opinion, representing as they do the thought and actions of a lifetime. But as judges we are neither Jew nor Gentile, neither Catholic nor agnostic. We owe equal attachment to the Constitution and are equally bound by our judicial obligations whether we derive our citizenship from the earliest or the latest immigrants to these shores.[29]

This is an extraordinary statement for the pages of the United States Reports; nothing else in all of those volumes, so far as I have read in them, approaches this intense confessional tone. But Frankfurter denied that there was anything "personal" about this statement. In his diary he recorded his response to Justice Murphy's plea "as a friend" and "for your benefit" to delete these opening sentences:

> I said I could understand that a reference to the fact that I am a Jew would be deemed to be personal if I drew on that fact as a reason for enforcing some minority rights. . . . But I do not see what is "personal" about referring to the fact that although a Jew, and therefore naturally eager for the protection of minorities, on the Court it is not my business to yield to such considerations, etc.[30]

There is a sharp line, a disjunction as he sees it, between Frankfurter the person and Frankfurter the judge. For one to become the other, indeed, this line must be drawn. In this formula there is no room for an empathic understanding between judge and litigant based on the judge's personal identifications. Thus the judge guards himself against favoritism, against prejudicial bias in favor of "people like himself." But if this judge's personal experiences and sympathies lean toward those who are "vilified and persecuted," as Frankfurter put it, there is considerable risk that rigorous exclusion of this empathic identification will push this judge into an alliance with the vilifiers and persecutors. Brandeis protected himself from this trap by building from this identification with oppressed outsiders toward a judicial role as their advocate, an instrument of their acknowledged social inclusion. Frankfurter—perhaps because identification with alien outsiders was rawer and more exposed for him than for Brandeis—excluded any such special understanding from his self-definition as a judge.

The most Frankfurter would extend to outsiders was an invitation to join the inner circle on the same terms and at the same costs that he had accepted. This, as Danzig has suggested, was the alternative Frankfurter was content to offer the Jehovah's Witness children—that they would find ready acceptance if they became full-fledged Americans (as he had done) by turning away from their alien language and idiosyncratic beliefs.[31] This was also the role Frankfurter saw for himself as a judge in the race segregation cases. There was an almost precise parallel between Frankfurter's passage from alien to citizen and the claims then articulated by Negro spokesmen for assimilation into the American mainstream.[32] Because segregation laws visibly blocked such assimilation, they violated the "fundamental values" that Frankfurter saw as the essence of American society for himself.

Frankfurter would not have said that his personal experience as an immigrant and a Jew was irrelevant to his conception of himself as a judge. I surmise that he believed his successful passage from alien to fully assimilated citizen gave him special insight as a judge into fundamental American values because he embodied those values in his own experience. He drew no protective mandate or special sympathy for outsiders, however, from this experience. He instead derived a mandate zealously to protect the values and status of insiders, such as he had become.

The irony of this special zeal occasionally struck even Frankfurter himself; in his reminiscences, he told of a question he posed at social encounter in 1940 to an isolationist senator who fervently opposed lend-lease aid to Great Britain:

> How is it that I who, as far as I know, haven't remotely a drop of English blood in me, who never heard the English language spoken, certainly never spoke a word of it until I was twelve, who never saw England until I was past thirty, have such a deep feeling about the essential importance of the maintenance of England, have such a sense of kinship professionally speaking with English institutions and feel that ours are so deeply related to their history and therefore am profoundly engaged in this cause with Englishmen, whereas you who I believe have nothing but English ancestry would on the whole view with equanimity the destruction of England?[33]

The senator, who was a direct descendant of one of the signers of the Declaration of Independence, responded that he, unlike Frankfurter, had "a memory of the red coats."[34] But for present purposes, Frankfurter's question is more interesting than the answer he received. Perhaps a better answer to that question is found in the special zeal of the convert. Whatever the answer, in his role as justice, Frankfurter saw himself specially obliged and specially qualified to discern the fundamental values of American society—as he put it in one case, "canons . . . which express the notions of justice of English-speaking peoples" (such as he had become).[35]

His qualifications and his judicial function went not only to discerning but to enforcing those values. Frankfurter is not unique among judges in prizing and demanding respect for law. But when he invoked this norm, it carried a notable stridency and, moreover, a stridently explicit conflation of respect for law and for judges who declare law. Both attributes were apparent in Frankfurter's concurrence in the 1947 *United Mine Workers* decision.[36] The Supreme Court majority concluded that a federal district court had statutory authority to issue an injunction against striking coal miners and the union's defiance of that injunction was accordingly punishable contempt of court. Two dissenting justices argued that the majority wrongly interpreted the statute and that, since the district court had no authority for its injunction, no punishment for contempt could be levied. Frankfurter took a separate position: while there was no statutory authority for its injunction, nonetheless even an unlawful court order must be obeyed until it is reversed by a higher court; therefore, he concluded, the union could be punished for contempt. Frankfurter's rhetoric on the way to this conclusion is instructive:

> The Founders knew that Law alone saves a society from being rent by internecine strife or ruled by mere brute power however disguised. . . . To that end, they set apart a body of men, who were to be the depositories of law, who by their disciplined training and character and by withdrawal from the usual temptations of private interest may reasonably be expected to be "as free, impartial, and independent as the lot of humanity will admit." So strongly were the framers of the Constitution bent on securing a reign of law that they endowed the judicial office with extraordinary safeguards and prestige.[37]

This was not simply Justice Frankfurter's conception of the judicial role. It was Felix Frankfurter's idealized vision of himself as a judge, "the depositor[y] of law . . . [with] disciplined character and training . . . endowed . . . with extraordinary safeguards and prestige." This is the voice of the quintessential insider. It is as if Frankfurter's passage from immigrant child who spoke no English to Supreme Court justice in full command of the language gave him special authority and responsibility as master grammarian.

But as much as Frankfurter strove to portray himself in this insider's status, as much as he sought to persuade himself that he had attained it, I believe that it was never comfortably his. Throughout his life he had aspired to this status—through his ebullient sociability and his "two hundred best friends," through his professional ascension to the faculty of the Harvard Law School and beyond. But when he finally reached the peak of this desire, as a justice of the United States Supreme Court, Frankfurter suddenly found himself unaccustomedly isolated: not isolated from the world at large, for he kept close ties there, but isolated within the Court, among his brethren.

Frankfurter arrived with the expectation on all sides that he would become the intellectual and spiritual leader of the new Court that Franklin Roosevelt was reconstructing on the ruined battlements of the old.[38] Frankfurter's opinion in *Gobitis,* speaking for eight members of the Court to delineate the proper judicial role in upholding the basic values of flag and country, was seen as an early token of that leadership.[39] But the *Gobitis* opinion was instead the beginning and the end of Frankfurter's acknowledged leadership on the Court.

Justices Black, Douglas, and Murphy soon regretted their concurring votes in *Gobitis* and abandoned Frankfurter's position on the specific issue raised. This abandonment was seen, by Frankfurter at least, as a stinging personal rebuke, a wholesale repudiation of his leadership. From *Gobitis* onward, Frankfurter was virtually consumed by a vitriolic anger toward his brethren.[40] Joseph Lash, who edited Frankfurter's diaries for publication and who was clearly sympathetic to him, made this prefatory observation: "Those who remember Frankfurter as a man of sweetness and vivacity, capable of intellectual detachment and impersonality, will be startled by some of the passages in these Diaries, passages that are full of wrath, contempt, superciliousness."[41] In his diaries and, I would surmise, in personal relations with his brethren on the Court, Frankfurter acted the leader abandoned by his followers, the lover spurned, the exile in his own country.

In the service of this bitter vision, Frankfurter repeatedly isolated himself on the Court with an almost perverse willfulness. The reversal of *Gobitis* illustrates the point. In his dissent from that reversal, Frankfurter explicitly sought comfort—"am fortified in my view," as he put it—from the fact that the flag salute controversy had been previously considered by the Court, not only in *Gobitis* but in earlier summary dispositions. "Every Justice—thirteen in all—who has hitherto participated in judging this matter," he said, had supported his position.[42] But seemingly eager as he was to amass support, to put himself in distinguished company, Frankfurter wrote his dissent itself in a manner that made it impossible for any other justice to join.

Two of Frankfurter's brethren, Justices Owen Roberts and Stanley Reed, still held to their votes supporting the prior result in *Gobitis*. But neither man joined Frankfurter's dissenting opinion; they wrote instead, and only, that they adhered "to the views expressed by the Court" in *Gobitis* and were of the opinion "that the judgment below should be reversed."[43] Those views were, of course, expressed for the Court by Frankfurter. But how could these willing allies now join Frankfurter's dissent when he launched it as "one who belongs to the most vilified and persecuted minority in history . . ."?

His willful isolation appeared in another dramatic instance much later—perhaps a more revealing instance because it was not in direct response to any repudiation of him. In *Cooper v. Aaron*[44] the Court was confronted by Governor Orval Faubus's overt challenge to its authority in ordering Arkansas state militia to bar black students from high school. The Court unanimously condemned Faubus's action. As one token of the enormity of Faubus's challenge and the gravity of the Court's response, the Court's opinion began with the proclamation that it was "by" each justice named individually rather than following the traditional format of identifying one justice to deliver "the opinion of the Court." The intended effect here was to emphasize that each justice in this case joined visibly and wholeheartedly in the common effort, that the Court was not simply unanimous but was *very* unanimous. This format was Frankfurter's specific suggestion, which his brethren approved.[45] But after this unanimous opinion was made public, Frankfurter announced to his colleagues that he intended to file his own separate concurring opinion.

As Chief Justice Earl Warren observed in his *Memoirs,* Frankfurter's action "caused quite a sensation" on the Court.[46] Justices Hugo Black and William Brennan declared that if Frankfurter took this step, they would enter their own statement dissenting from his filing; they circulated a draft dissent that conveyed their concern:

> The joint opinion of all the Justices handed down on September 29, 1958 adequately expresses the views of the Court, and [we] stand by that opinion as delivered. [We] desire that it be fully understood that the concurring opinion filed this day by Mr. Justice Frankfurter must not be accepted as any dilution or interpretation of the views expressed in the Court's joint opinion.[47]

Frankfurter in turn indicated that he would sign this statement as well as filing his own, since "it is impossible to conceive how anyone can reasonably find that my concurring opinion constituted a 'dilution'" of the joint opinion.[48] Public airing of this division, which would in itself have undermined the justices' shared wish for a unanimous appearance in *Cooper,* was averted with the help of a gently mocking draft statement circulated by Justice John Marshall Harlan ("concurring in part, expressing a *dubitante* in part, and dissenting in part").[49] Harlan stated that he concurred in the Court's original opinion "in which I have already concurred," that he doubted Frankfurter's "wisdom" in filing a separate opinion, but since he was "unable to find any material difference between" it and the Court's opinion, he dissented from the Black-Brennan opinion on the grounds "that it is always a mistake to make a mountain out of a molehill." Harlan ended this draft, "*Requiescat in pace.*"[50]

Peace prevailed, but not harmony on this matter. Frankfurter did file his separate opinion, and the others stayed silent. But Harlan's observation remains pertinent. There was no discernible difference between what Frankfurter said for himself and what the Court had said one week earlier. Why, then, did Frankfurter say anything? In a letter to a friend, Frankfurter later explained his rationale: "My opinion . . . was directed to a particular audience, to wit: the lawyers and the law professors of the South, and that is an audience which I was in a peculiarly qualified position to address in view of my rather extensive association, by virtue of my twenty-five years at the Harvard Law School, with a good many Southern lawyers and law professors."[51]

Beyond the extraordinary vanity of this observation, there is an unintended irony. Frankfurter spoke to his supposedly attentive audience to urge them to subordinate their personal views (on school integration) to a common effort that would vindicate the rule of law. In his opinion he observed, as the Court had also done, that the Little Rock school board had begun this effort, but was interrupted by Faubus's obstructionist tactics. But there was an unacknowledged tension in Frankfurter's separate opinion between his message and his medium. His opening words convey it:

> While unreservedly participating with my brethren in our joint opinion, I deem it appropriate also to deal individually with the great issue here at stake.
>
> By working together, by sharing in a common effort, men of different minds and tempers, even if they do not

> reach agreement, acquire understanding and thereby tolerance of their differences. This process was under way in Little Rock.[52]

This process was also under way among the justices of the Supreme Court in the intense collaboration and negotiation that had produced not only the joint opinion in *Cooper* but *Brown v. Board of Education*[53] itself. By filing his separate opinion, Frankfurter's willful disregard of his brethren's "working together," their "common effort," did not destroy the enterprise. But his action suggests that he had not adequately learned to "acquire understanding and thereby tolerance of . . . differences" as he enjoined on his former students in the South.

This entire episode of Frankfurter's separate opinion in *Cooper v. Aaron* suggests not so much his passion for standing alone on the Court as his compulsion to drive his brethren away. Frankfurter's diary entries from his Court tenure convey the same suggestion. For the most part, these entries were not private musings, but rather were selective verbatim transcriptions or paraphrases of Frankfurter's conversations with others. Frankfurter seemed convinced that he came off well in these recountings. But his conversations with other justices, as I read his version of them, were suffused with hectoring, condescending self-righteousness: only he understood the true issues at stake, only his motives were pure, only he embodied the noblest traditions of the Court from the days of the giants (after all, two of the tallest were his best friends, he untiringly observed).[54] Even a man as tolerant and companionable as Earl Warren apparently became alienated from Frankfurter, who first avidly wooed and then, when differences appeared between them, derisively dismissed him.[55]

Something, then, stopped Frankfurter from achieving his life's ambition—to feel fully at home as a member of the Court and, I would say, as a member of the American (or Anglo-

American) culture as he imagined it. There were external barriers; anti-Semitism, most notably, was a blatant obstructive force during his entire lifetime. But I believe there were also internal obstructions, a deep-rooted conception of himself that, much as he struggled against it, would not permit him to enter wholeheartedly into this insider's status. I have no direct evidence to support this speculation. But there is plausible indirect evidence to this end—most notably, his conduct on the Court, his self-defeating and isolating relations with his brethren, which obstructed his own explicitly chosen goals.

That evidence enables us to infer internal imagery from Frankfurter's external conduct. There is also evidence available for his internal imagery itself on this score. This evidence comes from his reminiscences, recorded when he was almost seventy-eight and had been a justice for some twenty years. Here is Frankfurter's explanation of why he chose not to become a judge—in this instance, a justice of the Massachusetts Supreme Court—when the position was offered to him in 1932:

> There were only two temptations that I had not to turn the nomination down. There were only two things that seemed to appeal to that part of my nature which is whimsical, why I should like to have accepted. In those days the seven members of the Supreme Judicial Court of Massachusetts went in lock step every day from where the court was sitting . . . to lunch at the Union Club in formal dress and top hat. I thought that would be an interesting thing—to go in lock step in top hat to the Union Club for lunch.
>
> The other consideration that appealed to me was the desire to satisfy [my] curiosity of the means that Chief Justice Rugg used whereby if a fellow dissented from an opinion, his opinion wouldn't be filed. How did he work it that grown men of independent position—life tenure—would suppress their views when presumably they

> felt them with sufficient strength to dissent. I was confident that he couldn't suppress any dissent of mine, and I just wondered how that would operate, but these two considerations didn't outweigh my sober convictions that the opportunities the Harvard Law School afforded me were more significant than even membership on the Supreme Judicial Court of Massachusetts.[56]

This, I believe, is a vivid characterization by Frankfurter of the conflicting impulses, the contradictory self-images, that barred him from wholeheartedly embracing the status either of insider or outsider throughout his mature life. Frankfurter's two reasons, his two temptations, for becoming a judge on the state supreme court are, of course, whimsically expressed. But they reveal the pattern nonetheless. His conflict was between the two reasons he cited—between marching "in lock step in top hat to the Union Club for lunch" and making sure that no one "suppressed any dissent" of his, a conflict between robing himself in the costumes and customs of his adopted and adored country and maintaining his independent identity, his critical distance from that society.

This same conflict, dressed in similar sartorial imagery, recurs in another episode Frankfurter recounted. In 1933 Frankfurter went to Oxford to spend the academic year as the George Eastman Visiting Professor. Here is his account of his first dinner party:

> That was a very memorable experience in my Oxford adventure. I went there in white tie. It was a formal dinner. Oh what a lovely green the college lawn was! My wife was ushered up to put her wraps down. I was waiting downstairs for her, and when she came down I said to her, "Marion, I'm sunk. I've disgraced myself and my country, Harvard—everything."
>
> "What's happened?"
>
> "It's terrible. Evidently I should have worn a[n academic] gown."

> A lot of guests came in, all of them gowned, even some of the ladies gowned. My wife said, "You'll have to make the best of it."
>
> It was a beautiful dinner. Those were still the days when there were four lovely glasses at each place, four courses of wine. It was a big party. This invitation was addressed to us as I was addressed the rest of the year, "The Eastman Professor." I had no name. I wasn't a person—"The Eastman Professor and Mrs. Frankfurter." You were known by your title. I did the best I could. Mrs. Lys was a very charming woman; indeed, a delightful, forth-putting hostess. The dinner was excellent, and I care about good food and wine. I'm something of a gourmet. But there they all were in gowns, and I was not dressed as I should have been, and that gnawed at me throughout the dinner. All things come to an end. We went home. That was that.[57]

The next day, Frankfurter went on, he encountered an English friend who congratulated him both for being properly dressed at the dinner and for learning Oxford etiquette so quickly; the local rule, it seemed, was that only those holding Oxford degrees might wear gowns on such occasions, while all other men had to wear white tie. "And so," Frankfurter said, "I started out propitiously, by good luck having complied with the mysteries of the custom of the country which you cannot find in any book at all."[58] Frankfurter then mentioned several other such Oxford rules, and observed:

> It was very strange, but I found myself being rather chauvinistic. I wanted to do everything better, or at least as well as my English friends there. . . . [But] all this was very perplexing, and nobody tells you anything. You know that you're not supposed to ask, and your pride prevents you from doing so. . . . You just have to smell it. This was all very trying, and my wife recalls—and it couldn't have been a fortnight, maybe a week or so after we got there—when I came home and said, "Mar-

> ion, to hell with it! I'm going to stop trying to please them. I'm going to just try to be what I am, and they'll have to put up with it."
>
> From that time on everything went smoothly. They didn't want an imitation Englishman. . . . I nailed my thesis of independence at the door of my house and said, "If you don't like it, to hell with you," and from that time on everything was hunkydory.[59]

At Oxford, of course, Frankfurter had it both ways. He was true to himself, and he pleased them anyway; indeed, as he saw it, that in itself pleased them: "The fact of the matter is that what they liked was my spontaneity."[60] I would surmise, as a general proposition, that Frankfurter had this best of both worlds for his entire career until he reached the Supreme Court. He was both properly attired and his own man, both insider and outsider, during his long tenure, in particular, at the Harvard Law School.

Just as Brandeis had conducted virtually a second full-time career as the "people's lawyer," Frankfurter also threw himself into public advocacy—some of which was passed directly from Brandeis on his appointment to the Court.[61] In this advocacy, Frankfurter invariably took the side of the oppressed, the outsider, as Brandeis had done. Frankfurter went the Paris Peace Conference as a lawyer-lobbyist for the Zionist Organization of America;[62] he was active on behalf of union organizers who, he alleged, were falsely accused of violence or were subjected to employer abuse; he argued in the Supreme Court to support the constitutionality of child labor laws and minimum wage laws for women.[63]

Through these activities, Frankfurter attracted a reputation as a radical, a "dangerous Bolshevik."[64] But Frankfurter maintained throughout that his advocacy was pure Americanism. In all of it, his central professed goal was to apply basic principles of American justice to protect those viewed as aliens by the corporate establishment. Frankfurter kept his balance between insider and outsider status by arguing to insiders on the basis of their own professed principles for the benefit of outsiders.

Frankfurter epitomized this in his portrayal of the reasons for his involvement in the Sacco-Vanzetti case. By the time the two men were executed, Frankfurter and Lawrence Lowell, the president of Harvard, had become the principal public antagonists in the case. At the appointment of the governor of Massachusetts, Lowell had conducted an inquiry into allegations of prosecutorial wrongdoing and judicial bias, and had concluded that the two men had been fairly convicted. But as Frankfurter saw it, the "essential" reality was that "Lawrence Lowell was incapable of seeing that two wops could be right and the Yankee judiciary could be wrong. . . . His crowd, the Yankees, were right, and the alien immigrants were what they were—pacifists and draft dodgers."[65]

But though Frankfurter saw this conflict at the heart of Sacco-Vanzetti, this was not the reason he claimed for entering the controversy. By his account, Frankfurter ignored the case (hardly even reading news accounts of it) for some five years after its inception, even though close friends urged him to express some opinion on it. He took active notice, Frankfurter said, only when an allegation appeared in the news that the prosecutor had induced a police witness to give misleading testimony at the trial and the prosecutor responded in an equivocal way to this charge. Frankfurter then resolved, he said,

> "I'm going to study this case and find out what it's all about." I was propelled and compelled by the something in me that revolted against this conduct of a district attorney. . . . If I hadn't been the kind of fellow I am, . . . if I didn't care passionately about the clean administration of justice in the United States, if I didn't feel as strongly as I do about law, it wouldn't have had that effect on me. . . . There was for me a far-reaching in-

> dictment of the disinterestedness that should guide the district attorney. . . . That outraged my sensibilities, outraged my whole conviction of what the administration of justice calls for, and my whole antecedents propelled me into action.[66]

Frankfurter did not say, in this retrospective account, whether his "whole antecedents" included the fact that he had been an "alien immigrant" like Sacco and Vanzetti and thus had special sympathy for them. To cite this reason explicitly would, however, have cast doubt on Frankfurter's "disinterestedness"—the failing for which he indicted the district attorney. Thus, he claimed, it was his "passionate" feelings about the "clean administration of justice in the United States" that "propelled and compelled" him into action—not his fellow-feelings for two oppressed immigrants.

But no one was fooled at the time, probably not even Frankfurter. The public significance of the controversy had already become, as Frankfurter saw, a conflict between Yankee and alien. Frankfurter had indeed already engaged in a bitter, "almost name-calling," dispute with Lowell about setting quotas to limit Jewish enrollment at Harvard.[67] Frankfurter must have understood that thrusting himself into public debate with Lowell on behalf of the "two wops" would be widely seen as a further expression of his earlier intra-university dispute on behalf of Jewish student applicants.

But even in that dispute Frankfurter portrayed himself as battling on behalf of American democratic, meritocratic values. And Frankfurter was, of course, correct in both cases. Traditionally espoused American values of equality and fairness were at stake, and "alien immigrants" would be the specific beneficiaries of the application of those values. If Frankfurter wanted it both ways—to be an apostle of Americanism while coincidentally favoring aliens like himself—it was easy enough for him to have both.

There was, however, even then—at least by Frankfurter's later recollection—some suggestion that both ways were not good enough for him. The suggestion appears in Frankfurter's account of Zechariah Chafee's defense in 1921 of his (Chafee's) advocacy on behalf of the Russian-Jewish aliens convicted of criminal sedition in *Abrams v. United States*.[68] Chafee was then on the faculty at the Harvard Law School; the university board of overseers had convened a special committee to investigate his conduct. Frankfurter recounted the proceedings:

> Chafee gave a calm, detailed, factual account of the *Abrams* case, stated the grounds why he thought the result was unfair. . . . When Chafee got through he said very quietly what I always thought was one of the most impressive sentences I ever heard in my life. He said, "I come of a family that have been in America from the beginning of time. My people have been business people for generations. My people have been people of substance. They have made money. My family is a family that has money. I believe in property and I believe in making money, but I want my crowd to fight fair."
>
> Then he sat down, and I tell you that really was a wonderful avowal of faith. More is said in that sentence than [in another more] famous credo . . . on what it means to be an American.[69]

However much Frankfurter might have admired Chafee's stance in 1921, and even (I would surmise) envied his qualifications for it, Frankfurter could not take the same high road. His family had not "been in America from the beginning of time"; he saw no advantage in exhorting "my crowd to fight fair." Frankfurter could only argue the point to Chafee's crowd; he was not a member of it. Throughout his Harvard years, Frankfurter remained thus poised between insider and outsider status—arguing to one side on behalf of the other, never identifying where his primary loyalties rested, but always insisting that the affiliational choice was unnecessary: a difficult, even dizzying, balancing act, which he executed with considerable agility.

But, by my estimation, when Frankfurter joined the Supreme Court in 1939, he lost his balance. His judicial office meant for Frankfurter that he now stood at the very center of American society as an embodiment of its values and traditions. Because he claimed that there was such a center, and that he could not only perceive it but had attained it, he was also prepared to force it on others who appeared as litigants in his Court. To be a Supreme Court justice was for Frankfurter a culminating expression of his passion for America, and the status itself seemed conclusive proof that the passion was reciprocated. His wish to achieve insider status, to find a home and an end to his personal exile, seemed finally to be within reach; and so he grasped it. But in this grasp he lost an essential aspect of his judgmental capacity; he became too single-minded, an overeager apologist for the existing order. He embraced an attitude to America that provided no critical distance for him in reaching judgment on his contemporary society or on himself.

Yet even at this personally culminating accession for Frankfurter, the long-sought prize of homecoming still eluded him. One episode at the very beginning of his tenure symbolizes the matter. James Landis, then dean of the Harvard Law School, recounted it (according to Joseph Lash in his biographical essay preceding Frankfurter's diaries):

> A gaffe in dress marked [Frankfurter's] first conference with his Brethren. He had the habit of wearing, unless in the classroom, "one of those little alpaca coats," when he was working, recalled Landis. So he came to the conference in an alpaca coat, only to discover the other justices fully dressed up. He was quite embarrassed, he later confided to Landis, and after the lunch break came back

> properly attired, only to see that Chief Justice Hughes had put on an alpaca coat.[70]

Frankfurter may have told the story to demonstrate Hughes's exquisite consideration and breeding in putting this new boy at ease, and it does indeed show this. But I would read more into it. Here was Frankfurter, at last eligible to dress up and march with his judicial brethren "in lock step in top hat to the Union Club for lunch," and he wore the wrong outfit. The chief justice then conformed his dress to that of this "latest immigrant to these shores" and thereby elegantly demonstrated his own social ease, his own unquestioned sense of belonging. And still, it turned out, Frankfurter dressed wrong.

Somewhere in this intricate minuet, Frankfurter had lost his bearings. Where was the "thesis of independence" that he had fixed as a marker on his doorpost in Oxford when he had previously been swept into a costume party? Where was his sense of self?

4

Pariah or Parvenu

Jews in Europe, Hannah Arendt has suggested, had only two social identities available to them from the beginning of the nineteenth century: pariah or parvenu. Notwithstanding the apparent promise of Enlightenment emancipation, European gentile society never offered Jews the option of unnoticed assimilation. This uneasy reception might not ineluctably have led to the Holocaust. It did mean, she observed, that Jews inevitably remained outsiders no matter how fervently they wanted to believe otherwise: hence they could occupy only the status of self-conscious pariah or parvenu.[1]

Frankfurter can readily be seen in Arendt's terms as parvenu: always charming, cajoling, seducing the widest possible circle of admirers, but never quite successful in finding the right chord, always somewhat strident, always a bit gauche.[2] Her account does not so easily fit Brandeis's marginality, his habitual stance at the boundary of insider/outsider status. Many of Brandeis's contemporaries did, however, see him as a perpetual outsider in ways that correspond to Arendt's account. This was the implication both of the scorn of the American bar leaders who opposed Brandeis's confirmation to the Court and of the admiration of those who saw Brandeis as a visionary social critic, a righteous prophet "wrapped [in] the mantle of Isaiah."[3]

The American relevance of Arendt's portrait of the Jew as

perpetual outsider cannot, moreover, be dismissed simply because a Brandeis or a Frankfurter attained the high social status of Supreme Court justice in this country. Arendt's depiction of the social significance of Benjamin Disraeli's Jewishness is instructive on this score, most particularly regarding Brandeis.[4] The "mysterious romance" in which Disraeli self-consciously cloaked himself, the Jewish racial identification that he invented for himself and its obviously fantastic character unrelated to any recognizable Jewish experience were less flamboyant in Brandeis. But these elements were present nonetheless in Brandeis's late embrace of Judaism only through Zionism and his romantic vision of an agrarian Jewish home of sturdy independent yeomen. Brandeis's attitudes to Zionism were only somewhat less tenuously rooted in his personal past or in the realistic possibilities of a Jewish future in Palestine than Disraeli's mythic views of himself as a Jewish nobleman and imperialist England as "the Israel of his imagination."[5]

Unlike Disraeli, Brandeis did not trade on his Jewish persona as an exotic qualification for entry into high society. But Brandeis's prophetic stance and his self-conscious distance from American society did correspond to a gentile vision of Jewish biblical tradition and separateness that gave social coherence and status to this role.[6] What Arendt observed in Disraeli we might also see in Brandeis, though directed toward a different goal: that both saw their Jewishness essentially through gentile eyes[7] (recall the Weizmann-bloc attack on Brandeis),[8] that both "had an admiration for all things Jewish that was matched only by . . . ignorance of them"[9] (recall Brandeis's confession on accepting the leadership of American Zionism),[10] and that their "unique rise to genuine popularity . . . [was] achieved through a policy of seeing only the advantages, and preaching only the privileges, of being born a Jew."[11]

Both Brandeis and Disraeli can thus be seen as Jews who

paradoxically attained high social status and yet remained indelibly Jewish and, as a consequence, social outsiders. Frankfurter, by contrast, did not emphasize (though he never denied) his Jewishness. Frankfurter's disinclination to ascribe any special significance to his Jewishness is not, however, the distinctive mark of the parvenu in Arendt's terms. Disraeli's example suggests that open emphatic avowal of Jewish identity can be consistent with parvenu ambition.

The contemporary social situation of Jews in America suggests the same proposition. Though many, perhaps even most, American Jews today readily identify themselves as such, this does not necessarily connote that they have abandoned parvenu aspirations in favor of self-conscious identification as social pariahs. Consider, in particular, the implications of the current concentration of Jews on American law school faculties.

The legal profession in America is still today the preferred path to political authority, as it was when Tocqueville wrote, one hundred fifty years ago, that lawyers were what passed for a "natural aristocracy" in American society.[12] For this reason alone, it is not surprising either that Jews were not quickly welcomed into the profession or that Jews eager for high social status would attempt the ascent through the legal profession. Since World War II, previous barriers to Jewish entry into the profession have been substantially lowered.[13] Contemporary Jewish representation within the profession is, however, much more concentrated on law school faculties than in other legal professional pursuits; in 1970, 25 percent of the faculties in American law schools were Jews, while among "elite" law schools Jews constituted 38 percent of the faculties.[14]

Brandeis himself made a special project of finding law faculty positions for young Jewish lawyers whom he regarded as particularly talented.[15] In 1929 he wrote this observation to Frankfurter (who was still the only Jew on the Harvard Law School faculty, a distinction he had held since his appointment in 1914):[16]

> It seems to me that a great service could be done generally to American law and to the Jews by placing desirable ones in the law school faculties. There is in the Jew a certain potential spirituality and sense of public service which can be more easily aroused and directed, than at present is discernible in American non-Jews. The difficulty which the Law Schools now have in getting able men may offer opportunities, not open in other fields of intellectual activity.[17]

Brandeis invoked here his characteristic conjunction of a romantic vision of Jewishness (its "spirituality and sense of public service") and a cool appreciation of practical possibilities (that law schools would have less "difficulty" in recruiting "able men" among Jewish lawyers because they were effectively barred from more lucrative professional opportunities available to their gentile brothers).

The immediate occasion for Brandeis's letter was his wish to enlist Frankfurter's assistance in finding a law school teaching position for his then clerk, Harry Shulman. Brandeis specifically mentioned in that letter that one faculty member at Yale had told him "that the right man there would find no opposition on the score of anti-Semitism." Shulman did in fact find a teaching position at Yale; and in 1953 he became dean of the Yale Law School, the first Jew to hold that post. During this interval the status of Jews in American law school faculties markedly changed. By 1971, when the Harvard Law School appointed its first Jewish dean, there were Jews in the dean's chair at Yale, Columbia, Pennsylvania, Berkeley, and UCLA.

This dramatic incursion of Jews into law school faculties, particularly in the elite schools that are privileged points of entry into the profession, might appear to signify full assimilation of Jews, the virtual ending of their outsider status. I would say, however, that this new social phenomenon reflects the continuation of a special social role for Jews—a role akin to the high status outsider that both Brandeis and Disraeli represented in their different ways. The basis for my supposition can be grasped through Isaiah Berlin's portrayal of the intellectual significance of the persistently alien status of Jews living among the gentile "tribes" of Europe: that strangers are especially acute observers of tribal mores.

> [They] become primary authorities on the natives; they codify their language and customs, they compose the tribe's dictionaries and encyclopedias, they interpret the native society to the outside world. . . . Hence the fantastic over-development of their faculties for detecting trends, and discriminating the shades and hues of changing individual and social situations, often before they have been noticed anywhere else. Hence, too, their celebrated critical acumen . . . their well-known genius for observation and classification, and explanation—above all for *reportage* in its sharpest and finest forms.[18]

Berlin's observation equally applies in America to the relation of law teachers (Jew or gentile) to the legal profession. The cultivation of the kind of acuity he describes is the hallmark of the academician within the legal profession. Jews have no monopoly on this capacity; they are, however, inclined toward it more by group ethnic experience than by the more individually diverse routes traveled by their gentile colleagues.

The current concentration of law teachers among Jewish lawyers may, of course, be a passing phenomenon; the next generation of Jewish lawyers may be scattered through the entire range of professional pursuits in the same proportions as their gentile colleagues. The next generation of American Jews may, indeed, move away from the professions of law, medicine, and accountancy (where they are currently clustered) into conventionally undifferentiated business pursuits.[19] This next generation may no longer feel the need to protect itself through the same eager pursuit of formally recognized professional credentialing, the legacy that this generation of

American Jews inherit from their parents' experience of extensive overt discriminations in the gentile world. This social foundation for the continued experience and conscious awareness of outsider status may, in short, soon end for Jews as such in American life.[20]

Even if overt discrimination against Jews does wholly vanish from American life, however, and even if American Jews come to see their religious affiliation as carrying no different separatist significance than membership in one of the Protestant denominations, American Jews will not shake loose from outsider status. This sense of alien status, of homelessness in America, will persist for Jews because this very sense pervades American social life. Homelessness, alienation, has become the only social status truly available in American society. Jews are specially sensitized to this status, and thus have readier access to self-conscious acknowledgment of it, as a result of their specific historic experiences. This status has, however, become the universal American experience.

Many Jews in Europe and America have, of course, denied the social reality of their alien status. Their denial did not, however, alter the fundamental social fact that they remained outsiders. This is what Hannah Arendt meant when she posited that European Jews had only a limited social repertoire available to them—to act as either pariah or parvenu; because they were denied membership in any homeland, they were barred from true insider status. Arendt's formulation applies today in American society not simply to Jews but to everyone: only the roles of pariah and parvenu are available. There is no social role of assimilated insider for anyone; there is no such reliable, unquestioningly secure status in American social life.

This is the basic reason that Jews during the past generation have received such ready entry into American law faculties. I have already identified many reasons why Jews seek these positions; the question remains, however, why law schools should be so open to the extraordinary Jewish immigration into their ranks that has occurred during the past generation. The answer comes, I believe, from the implicit awareness that has grown within the American legal academy that Jews, by virtue of their historic experience, are specially adept at understanding and constructing social rules based on the fundamental fact that insider status is barred to them. In this sense, Jews have become particularly acute observers of, and illuminating figures in, the contemporary social experience of all Americans.

The underlying forces that have eroded insider status in America did not suddenly appear full-blown during the past generation. These forces were evident from the founding days of the Republic and even earlier. American society has had the unique experience of creating itself from the first moments of immigration to the New World. Social authority in this country has always had a self-consciously constructed aspect to it, much more so than Old World patterns; America virtually invented the idea that written constitutions could form the basis for social organization, that society could be founded at a distinct historical moment rather than emerging organically from some misty tribal past.

American society has often tried to invent this past for itself, as the iconization of the Constitution testifies. But this enshrining effort has repeatedly been undermined by the individualist premises on which even the Constitution itself rests: the idea that "We the People" chose, as free individuals, to affiliate. This premise of individual voluntarism, of social life based on a contract among free individuals, has always carried an implication of tenuous social bonding. The word *individualism* itself was coined by Tocqueville to describe this unique social phenomenon—the absence of unquestioningly habituated social bonding—that he observed in America.

We have frequently celebrated our "rugged individualism" as the basis of the American sense of freedom, of bold venturing to uncharted frontiers. A contrapuntal theme has, however, virtually always accompanied this celebration—a sense of loss, of rootlessness. This counterpoint has usually been more muted than self-congratulation for our freedoms; but the theme of longing for an imagined lost state of harmonious social relations was present, as various historians have observed, from colonial times through the nineteenth century.[21] (The recurrence of this theme may indeed reflect, as Freud has suggested, a deep psychological imperative that inevitably leads people to portray the universal experience of development from infancy to adulthood as a progression from reliably nurturant unity to vulnerable alienation.)[22]

Whatever the social or psychological sources of this recurrent concern regarding social alienation, it is an intense preoccupation of our own times. This concern frequently appears in these very terms, in publicly voiced complaints about massed anonymity, rootlessness, and personal vulnerability in American society.[23] The "broken home" is a common experience of our time, as shown both by the dramatically increased divorce rate of recent years[24] and the persistent high frequency with which Americans change residences.[25]

Social alienation is, moreover, a dominant theme in our public life. Consider, most notably, the significance of the Civil Rights movement following World War II. Blacks had been oppressed in this country before that time; the abolition of slavery after the Civil War had not ended their oppression. But by the end of World War II, the oppression of blacks had become newly visible. Some have explained this new visibility by changes among blacks themselves, in their increased education and economic status, coupled with increased migration to the North.[26] Blacks were certainly now taking new initiatives to protest their oppression. At this same time, however, there was a new readiness among whites to see the oppression of blacks—a receptivity that itself encouraged black protest.

This white receptivity was based on an unarticulated fellow

feeling that had not previously existed—a fellow feeling that both defined and was articulated by the black protests. Blacks presented themselves, and were seen by whites, as alienated from the privileged inner circle of American society—as homeless in the only land they could claim, torn from their roots in Africa and shut off from access to secure rootedness in America. This was the central evil of race segregation as blacks portrayed and whites understood it.

This portrayal implicitly flattered and reassured whites. In this social portrait, blacks sought access to an American mainstream, an inner core of safety and prosperity—a goal that was thereby depicted as worth pursuing. Whites now felt unaccustomed sympathy with, and were therefore prepared to hear, the black complaints of oppression because whites themselves felt alienated, shut away from access to some secure homeland. At this same time whites took comfort from, and therefore gave increasing credence and visibility to, the black complaints implying that this safe place existed and that whites already had privileged access to it.

Blacks' willingness to flatter and to comfort whites was epitomized in Martin Luther King, Jr.'s famous dream, where not only blacks but "all God's children" would achieve freedom by joining together in racial brotherhood.[27] This inclination among blacks dramatically receded, however, after the early 1960s. In the succeeding phase of the movement, blacks invested racial separatism with new approbation and fervor. They invented a new designation for themselves as "blacks," rejecting the appellations "Negro" and "colored" as merely the whites' names for black people. One explanation for this new direction among blacks is that most whites refused to yield their privileged status in the American "mainstream," and blacks ultimately turned away in frustration and anger. White resistance to black demands was indeed powerful and remains so. But I am not persuaded that this resistance is the whole explanation, or even a major portion of it, for this new development among blacks.

Black separatism appears to me much more rooted in the contemporary incoherence of the "mainstream" idea itself, of the ideology that offers a unitary insider status, a safe and prideful locus of identity to anyone as an unhyphenated American. Black claims for inclusion in the American mainstream had achieved such credence and prominence because these misgivings were already shared by whites. It is thus not surprising that the supposed reward of access to insider status could not indefinitely retain a lustrous appeal. American blacks turned to find roots among themselves and in an African past because they sensed that neither they nor anyone could be firmly rooted in a contemporary American homeland.

Race relations are not the only setting where this social imagery has taken hold in American public life. Gender relations have followed the same course, building, often self-consciously, on the vocabulary employed by the black Civil Rights movement. In the 1960s, the first phase of the contemporary resurgence of the gender issue, feminists demanded access to the insider status of male privilege and power. As with blacks, women identified their oppression as exclusion from this mainstream; their inclusion would thus bring women's liberation.[28] Women's claims for liberating inclusion in male preserves were, moreover, both implicitly flattering and explicitly threatening to men, just as black claims both flattered and threatened whites.

In the rhetoric of the women's movement the threat was more prominently vocalized than the flattery; but this was only the surface appearance. Power, privilege, and authority were scarce commodities for most men in America of the 1960s. The main threats to male pride and safe status did not come from women but from the complexity and anonymity of the marketplace, from a structure of economic and social relations apparently beyond anyone's capacity to control or even clearly understand. The women's liberation movement identified the virtues of self-determination with male status (and with participation in the marketplace economy) at a time when most men had reason to fear that these virtues were unattainable for them. It was safer for men to acknowledge the threatening aspect of women's claims for access to male privilege than to admit that this privilege felt empty; safety was indeed offered to men by the flattery implicit in women's valuation of male status.

As with the Civil Rights movement, this flattery was not sustained. Separatism among women, the claimed virtues of "sisterhood," was one instrument to this end; but unlike black separatism, this development in the women's movement was not their most powerful statement devaluing the very concept of insider status. The most dramatic and unsettling aspect of the women's movement was its visible abandonment of the ideal of domesticity, of a safe haven from a cruelly impersonal world, that had been the basic rationale for the social differentiation of male/female roles in our society.

Many generations of women had suffered under the constraints imposed by this domestic ideal. Feminist advocates had identified these oppressions as such during all of this time.[29] Early feminist complaints of oppression were disregarded, however, because substantial numbers of women and men perceived compensating advantages in the social valorization of the domestic role, the special worth they felt in the creation of this warm hearth, this safe home base in a world of threatening vulnerability.[30] The feminist complaints of oppression were not new in the 1960s; the new element was the widely perceived devaluation of the domestic role.

Whatever the social and economic forces that led to this devaluation, the critical fact is that it had occurred; a newly receptive audience was available, among both women and men, who no longer saw much social value in the fuzzy image of domestic tranquility that had previously given worth to women's "special place" in the home. The compensating domestic ideal had eroded for women; there was now only constraint and oppression in domesticity.

From men's perspective, the idea of "home" had also lost whatever force it previously possessed to protect them in the marketplace. To be sure, many men and women still found great satisfaction in domestic life. But their achievement was "merely personal"; it did not correspond to, or draw special support and force from, a coherent social ideal. Domesticity had lost its salience as a social ideal, as a reliably safe retreat from the vulnerabilities and oppressions of social life generally. In this sense, men saw oppression everywhere, with no compensating respite in a safe home.

Women saw the same pervasive oppression, though not in this unrelievedly bleak way. At the first stage of the contemporary feminist movement, women could still imagine some safe haven elsewhere—in the marketplace, in the mainstream, on an equal footing with men of power and privilege—perhaps because their vision had been more restrictively focused on the home and its oppressions. In the succeeding stage of the feminist movement, many adherents (both women and men) advocated the introduction of domestic values into the marketplace—to replace competition with cooperation, authoritarian orders with voluntarist persuasion, cold-hearted bosses with sensitively attentive personnel managers.[31]

This program represented the extension of the ideal of domesticity from the home to all social relations, and as a practical matter, it may not succeed in transforming marketplace relationships. The wide currency of the program and its confounding of home and marketplace testify, however, to the erosion in our contemporary culture of the once-clear delineations of the ideal of domesticity, to the tenuousness of the idea that anyone in America today has access to a safe home. (The evolution of this programmatic domesticity among feminists also ironically suggests that a significant segment of the modern feminist movement is not rejecting the old ideal of a special domestic role for women. These feminists are instead extending that role beyond the confined boundaries of the "home" because this social space is no longer seen as an adequate locus for the domesticating mission.)

These terms of public discourse have not been limited during the past generation to race or gender relations. Homelessness has become the commonly held fear and the shared status of all Americans. During the past thirty years, it has been hard to find anyone who claims to be fully at home in American society; the most popular self-depiction has been membership in some vulnerable minority. This is true not only for blacks and women (and various ethnic and religious groups, gays, disabled people, elderly people) who have self-consciously embraced the civil rights paradigm of oppressed outsider status. It is also true for those claiming to be "true insiders"—as middle Americans or the "moral majority"—who nonetheless speak in such embattled terms, at times almost of paranoid intensity, as to suggest that they too imagine themselves oppressed by some vast and unjustly powerful force (albeit a numerical minority).[32]

The interplay among various groups, each staking claim to, and at the same time fearing, the status of oppressed outsider, has been vividly symbolized in the recent public discourse about mentally ill people. During the first half of this century, professional and popular opinion were virtually united in viewing large geographically isolated residential institutions as the best possible place for mentally ill people. Beginning in the 1950s, this viewpoint changed dramatically: large institutions were unmasked as horrifying, dehumanizing "snakepits"; mentally ill people were reconceived as unjustly (and untherapeutically) excluded from the mainstream of community life.[33] The mentally ill, that is, also became the embodiment of the oppressed outsider, excluded from the nurturant home where the majority of Americans lived "safe and sane." At the same time, this majority acknowledged that mentally ill people were not so different from them as to justify this policy of rigorous exclusion and isolation. (Indeed, many people now spoke of mental illness as a fiction invented by the majority to create a comforting, but equally false, construct of normality.)[34]

In the 1960s the dominant professional and popular forces recanted their old policy toward mentally ill people. Community residence for all such people became the new watchword. Large isolated mental institutions were closed; the population in such institutions declined from almost 560,000 at the end of 1955 to little more than 115,000 by 1985.[35] Mentally ill people did not, however, find the nurturant homes in the American communal mainstream that had been promised for them. Many became residents in squalid, dangerous single-room-occupancy hotels in urban slums. Many simply wandered the streets by day and slept in the streets at night, thus forming the core of a new class of Americans that have become visible as such during the 1980s: the homeless.

The same story thus unfolded in relations between mentally normal and mentally ill people that had evolved in race and gender relations during approximately this same time. The mentally normal majority discovered in the 1950s that they were not as different from the mentally ill minority as they had believed (and hoped). Mentally ill people were henceforth promised equal membership in the American community—that is, given no more protection, no more nurturance and warmth, no more stability and sanity than anyone else in the American mainstream. The mentally ill were thus assimilated to the normal status of homelessness in America: except, of course, that they remained more visibly homeless than anyone else. The majority could thus continue to see itself as powerful because of the visible existence of this vulnerable minority; this majority could still take some comfort that they were clearly different from the mentally ill, from the "truly homeless" who slept on the streets.

This cruel, ironic twist in the evolution of this publicly enacted parable arises from a central imperative in the psychology of any society where homelessness is pervasively experienced. The very idea that a society might be characterized by such pervasive alienation is deeply paradoxical. Such a society can have no clearly defined criteria of inclusion or exclusion for its membership: a society of outcasts is a contradiction in terms. The members of this self-contradictory entity experience the contradiction as a profound uncertainty about the basis for, and solidity of, their attachments to one another. They are not able to construct inclusive/exclusive criteria that reassure those seemingly rewarded with insider status. In its palpable brittleness, this insider status itself holds as much concern as comfort for its possessors, a concern akin to (if not more confusing and unsettling than) the experience of those explicitly excluded from this status.

Mutual uncertainty and mistrust thus arise from the abstract logical contradiction inherent in conceiving a society composed of outcasts. Gnawing doubts among those apparently blessed with insider status are unavoidable even in moments of seeming social calm. This uncertainty is, moreover, magnified when any overt social conflict disrupts the uneasy calm. In a competitive rush to protect the (always) embattled insider status, to make its boundaries clearer and somehow more secure, the categorization of outsiders is more expansively defined as such.

This is the inner logic that led, as Arendt saw, from the imposition of special disabilities to the denaturalization to the physical destruction of Jews in Nazi Germany: a tenuously bonded society demarks a specially visible group of outsiders in order to create a distinctive class of insiders; but the intrinsic uncertainty of the boundaries of this "no-man's land" leads the putative insiders toward a literal depopulation of that fearfully imagined realm.[36] Orlando Patterson has sketched this same dynamic in his comparative survey of the structural significance of slave status—slavery, as he put it, was "social death." Slavery supported a communal sense of social vitality, of life and safety, among the "free" by creating a boundary status of "slave" occupied by people who, though physically alive, were socially dead.[37]

If I am correct that American society today is characterized by a pervasive sense of homelessness, and if the vicious dynamic of death and enslavement would take hold as a result of this widely shared feeling, then we face an urgent question: How can this dynamic reliably be averted in America?

I find a possible answer to this question in the contrasting conceptions of social authority that Louis Brandeis and Felix Frankfurter exercised as Supreme Court justices. Because both men linked their conceptions of the judicial role to their self-perceptions as outsiders, we can discern in their conduct the same sets of responses likely when any social outcast finds himself in a position of great power. If no one in America today is able to perceive himself or herself in social terms except as a homeless outsider, then the outcast in power is the modal embodiment of authority in our time. What had seemed exceptional, even paradoxical, in Brandeis's or Frankfurter's time —Jewish (which is to say, alien or outcast) justices of the Supreme Court—has thus now become the rule.[38]

If the Jewish experience of homelessness has assumed more general relevance for American society, so that Brandeis's and Frankfurter's self-conceptions offer a generally applicable contemporary lesson, this experience does not clearly demonstrate the importance of this lesson in America. This is because Jewishness does not carry the same social signification in this country as it has in Europe. The status of Jews was a central, explicit, and recurrent issue of broad political concern in Europe during the nineteenth and twentieth centuries.[39] The "Jewish question" never attracted the same intense attention in America; the status of Jews here had more in common with concerns about American reception of other latter-day immigrant groups.[40]

The most direct American parallel to the convulsive "Jewish question" in Europe was the long-fought-out status of blacks in the nineteenth and twentieth centuries. In order to understand the full significance for American society of the contrasting roles offered by Brandeis and Frankfurter, we must first describe how the national experience of black slavery served as the American counterpart of the dynamic that led in Europe to the physical destruction of the Jews.

In the late eighteenth century, when the Republic was established, Southern as well as Northern whites widely believed that the institution of slavery would gradually disappear.[41] Within two generations, however, this belief had been jettisoned in the South. Formal boundaries between slave and free status were depicted with intensified rigidity and more thoroughgoing racism in matters such as restrictions on voluntary manumissions by slaveholders and prohibitions against literacy education for slaves.[42] This new rigor (interfering, incidentally, with the autonomy of individual slaveholders over their slaves) reflected an increasingly adamant insistence by Southern white society that its coherence depended on the maintenance and sharper delineation of slave status. This increasing rigidity and its underlying uncertainty fed a mounting and magnified fear among Southern whites at the potential threat of Northern white abolitionists to their peculiar institution.[43]

At the same time complementary uncertainties in the North led to its increasing insistence (which fed Southern white paranoia) that black slavery be rigidly confined to the South in order to demark a clear-cut distinction between "free" and "slave" labor and status in the social experience of Northern whites. This was the symbolic implication of the Northern demand for the geographic exclusion of slavery from the territories (a demand that had much stronger popular support in the North than abolitionism).[44] It seemed clear at the time, and has become even clearer in retrospect, that there were no immediate "practical" implications to this demand, since slavery was unlikely to spread, much less thrive, in any of the disputed territories.[45] The Northern demand for containing slavery and the contradictory Southern demand for the universal legitimacy of slavery was at its heart a struggle about social symbolism.

The Civil War resulted, I believe, from the inability among whites in the North and South to fix a settled status on blacks that did not palpably undermine the differently defined, but equally uncertain, sense of "freedom" and "power"—the social depiction of insider status—within these two regions. The Supreme Court's decision in *Dred Scott,*[46] that blacks could not be citizens of the United States, ratified the Southern demand that slaves be symbolically fixed outside the Union. Northern whites did not welcome the physical presence of blacks in their region; but the symbolic exclusion of blacks as a perpetually enslaved laboring class was widely perceived in the North as somehow the first step toward the enslavement of white laborers throughout the federal Union.[47]

This Northern white fear was not appeased by the withdrawal of the South from the Union. If anything, secession seemed to intensify these fears—as if any outsider status, visibly depicted as such, had become intolerable for Northern whites, whether that status was marked as "slave" or as "rebel." Why, after all, was the North not willing to accept the Confederate states' secession?

Northern commitment to keep hold of the South in order to abolish slavery is surely not the answer to this question. On the very eve of the Civil War, both Lincoln and the Congress were prepared to disclaim any abolitionist intentions in order to preserve the Union. On March 2, 1861—two days before Lincoln's inauguration and just a month before the bombardment of Fort Sumter—Congress, by more than a two-thirds vote, sent a proposed constitutional amendment to the states that irrevocably protected the institution of slavery where then extant. If ratified, it would ironically have been the Thirteenth Amendment. Lincoln explicitly endorsed this proposed amendment in his inaugural address.[48]

On the eve of the war, moreover, there was considerable support in the North for the proposition that Southern states, if they were foolish enough to secede, should be permitted to "go in peace." (The phrase is Horace Greeley's, published in his influential *New York Tribune* three days after Lincoln's election).[49] David Potter has suggested that the offer was not seriously meant, since most Northerners (including Greeley himself) simply could not believe that the secessionist threats were substantial.[50] When secession did in fact come, the offer was promptly withdrawn, even by Greeley. But this small episode in itself only deepens the mystery: why should the North fight, and with such ferocity, to maintain a political Union with such obviously unwilling and hostile partners? It is not enough simply to suggest, as Potter seems to do, that the North unthinkingly backed itself into the conflict by rejecting both compromise and voluntary separation, thereby making war inevitable, though not intended as such.[51] The question remains why voluntary separation was not accepted by the North, particularly after the high costs involved in maintaining the Union became clear.

The most plausible direction for answering this question would seem to come from attending to Northern concerns about growing disorder in the North itself, reflected in Lincoln's famous 1837 lyceum speech condemning "the increasing disregard for law which pervades the country," including vigilantism, mob violence, and those who hoped for "total annihilation of government." As Eric Foner has observed, Lincoln conflated "law, order, and union"—most starkly revealed in his 1861 inaugural declaration that "plainly, the central idea of secession, is the essence of anarchy."[52] This growing concern for the maintenance of social order and corresponding intolerance for social deviance of various stripes was clearly reflected in the creation of new forms of prisons and mental institutions for confinement and reform of deviants in the decades before the Civil War.[53] The Southern secessionists, from this perspective, were yet another eruption of deviance, of social alienation, which must be suppressed in order to reassert the solidity and reliability of the social order for everyone.

The symbolic struggle with the South thus brought into clearer focus for the North the fact that it had begun to see itself as a society composed of aliens, of outcasts. In its more thoroughgoing commitment to individualism and equality, and the concomitant tenuousness of social bonding implicit in that commitment, Northern white society had become a prototype for the common twentieth-century sensibility of social alienation. The war waged by the North also—I would say, as a consequence—became a prototype for the common twentieth-century experience in the unrestrained character of its destructive violence. The American Civil War outstripped all recorded precedents, not only in the numbers of combatants killed as a proportion of the adversaries' general population, but even more notably in its indiscriminate involvement of civilian populations in hostile fire and in its aim of total and unconditional surrender of the adversary, the utter destruction of its organized social identity.[54]

This unprecedented incapacity to contain the violence of this conflict was related to interlocking paradoxes in the combatants' conceptions of their war aims. On the Northern side, there was the paradox that fighting for the preservation of the Union required the North to reject the principle of self-determination on which the Union had been founded and on which Southern whites based their secession;[55] the North thus waged war to impose an involuntary submission on Southern whites, a dominative relationship itself akin to slave status. On the Southern side, there was the paradox that Southern whites fought for their rights to self-determination, in whose name they centrally claimed the right to deprive blacks of self-determination. Both of these paradoxes reflected the incoherence of the conception of the bases for social bonds in both North and South, the tenuousness, if not ultimately the internal contradiction, implicit in the attempt to conceive a society as wholly composed of self-determining—that is to say, alienated—individuals.[56]

The tenuousness of this conception, and its inner impetus toward demarking some group as more outcast than other outcasts, some as more alien than others who are "merely" alienated from one another, found its fullest expression in the aftermath of the Civil War and in its ultimate paradox: that black slavery was somehow the cause of the war and yet the actual conditions of blacks were ultimately irrelevant to the resolution of hostilities. For most Northern whites, the conceptual abolition of slave status adequately achieved their goals (whether they had been avowed abolitionists or merely territorial "free soil" advocates) without any need for sustained attention to the subsequent condition of the slaves actually freed.[57] The post-bellum regime of formal abolition sufficiently allayed the prior suspicion among Northern whites that if Southern laborers were slaves, then they too were slaves; that this visibly subordinated status was shared with blacks rather than clearly differentiated from their own status as "free labor."[58]

For post-bellum Southern whites, locked as they were in daily contact with blacks, formal abolition of slavery brought no conceptual or practical advantage.[59] They devised other means, however, to differentiate themselves from blacks' status through the reimposition of racial subordination that followed Reconstruction—a subordination whose visible expression in the "merely social" etiquettes of race segregation appeased Northern sensibilities by masking the continued centrality of the employment relationship in Southern black servitude. By thus abolishing "slave labor" and yet evolving a regime of black "social" subordination, the reconstituted

Union demarked a visible class of outsiders that gave white insiders, North and South, some reason to believe that they were not also subordinates, outcasts, aliens.

By the end of the nineteenth century, this belief had less plausibility for the growing masses of white workers in both the North and the South. As C. Vann Woodward has shown, Southern state policies increasing both the scope and the rigidity of race segregation had the effect of diverting white laborers from conceiving common class interests with blacks from which a broad-based populist movement might have grown.[60] Race thus remained, and was reinforced as, the central depiction of the boundary between insider and outsider in the South.

For the North, however, a racial demarcation would not serve the same purposes. Economic class differentiation between capitalist and worker became the central depiction for social conflict in the North.[61] Around the time of the Civil War, the social categories of "worker" and "owner" were blurred in the North; the dominant agricultural modality was small-tract farmers working their own land, while nonagricultural production workers either were self-employed or predominantly saw themselves as "apprentices" who could ultimately become self-employed.[62] By the end of the century, however, the owner/worker categories had become rigidly distinct in nonagricultural modes, while farmers increasingly saw themselves as subordinated workers "owned" by banks and other creditors.[63]

This was the social framework within which Brandeis's generation saw their world and against which Brandeis himself etched his conception of the judicial role.

5

A Jewish Court

Economic class conflict was at the center of Brandeis's concern. As acute as Brandeis's appreciation was for the predicament of the outsider in this context, however, and as powerfully as he gave voice to this perspective in his judicial work, Brandeis did not extend this understanding or conceive this judicial role on behalf of black people. On the occasions when the Court addressed the status of blacks, Brandeis remained silent; he joined, for example, in the unanimous decisions reaffirming the constitutionality of segregated education and interstate transportation facilities.[1] There were occasional Court decisions during Brandeis's tenure aimed at ameliorating black oppression in the criminal justice system, white primaries, segregated graduate education, and enforcement of restrictive housing covenants.[2] Brandeis joined in these decisions, but he took no visible leading role in their advocacy; he was within the Court consensus but not ahead of it.

Before joining the Court, Brandeis even occasionally spoke as if issues of economic oppression had somehow supplanted questions of race oppression. Thus in 1911 Brandeis publicly proclaimed:

> We have no place in the American democracy for the money king, not even for the merchant prince. We are confronted in the twentieth century, as we were in the

> nineteenth century, with an irreconcilable conflict. Our democracy cannot endure half free and half slave. The essence of the trust is a combination of the capitalist, by the capitalist, for the capitalist.[3]

In 1912 he similarly characterized the problem of nonvested employee pensions, which employers used to inhibit both union activities and employee mobility,[4] as "our new peonage." There is no mention in his public or private papers that I have encountered, however, acknowledging the persistence of the old peonage at this same time.

Brandeis was certainly not alone among his generation in his disregard for the pervasive oppression of blacks in the South and elsewhere. In other matters, however, he did not chart his course from the direction taken by others. Brandeis's inattention to the status of blacks was a considerable shortcoming in his vision.[5] I would say, moreover, that Brandeis's inattention here was inconsistent with his own conception of the judicial role in a democratic polity.

Brandeis never gave a comprehensive account of his judicial role conception. A generalized principle was, however, implicit in Brandeis's attitude toward economic class conflict. Even if Brandeis himself failed to give consistent application to this principle, as in race matters, the principle itself is a more important and reliable guide for contemporary action than Brandeis's lapses from it. Indeed, as we shall see, the principle that I discern in Brandeis's judicial position on economic class conflict was given generalized application in the work of the Warren Court.

Brandeis believed that the central issue of his time was a "revolutionary" change in American economic class relations. "[W]ithin the last fifty years, we have passed through an economic and social revolution which affected the life of the people more fundamentally than any political revolution known to history," he stated in 1916, just one month before his nomination to the Court.[6] As he saw it, a class of "new peons" had arisen:

> Half a century ago nearly every American boy could look forward to becoming independent as a farmer or mechanic, in business or professional life; and nearly every American girl might expect to become the wife of such a man. To-day most American boys have reason to believe that throughout life they will work in some capacity as employees of others, either in private or public business; and a large percentage of the women occupy like positions.[7]

These observations were directly relevant, though diametrically opposed, for Brandeis and his brethren on the Court in the roles they saw for themselves as judges. The Court majority drew for itself the lesson that employers were the direct and sole heirs of the prized status of independent entrepreneur, the modal American insider; that employees were dependents, subordinates, unpropertied outsiders; and that the central social role of judges was to protect the insiders against expropriative assault by the outsiders.[8] Brandeis by contrast found himself usually allied with these outsiders; but this alliance was only a strategic means to advance his fundamental goal, which was to obviate this social distinction between insider and outsider.

Brandeis was no John the Baptist wandering the desert inveighing against the irredeemable evils of organized social life. He aspired to a more practical prophecy. He combined a lawyerly attention to the detailed workings of existing institutions with the hope that in the patient emendation of these detailed institutional mechanics, his transcendent social vision would be brought toward closer realization—a vision in which the lion and lamb of industrial conflict would lie down together in peace, a secular Kingdom of Heaven.

Brandeis maintained this vision by standing at the social

margin between those who were comfortably included and those bitterly outside, and he pleaded for the disappearance of the distinction. This basic plea was the reason in conceptual terms that "bigness," that large-scale organization, was such a curse for Brandeis. If social relations could be dissolved into their component parts, into individuals confronting one another only as such, then the galling division between inside and outside would disappear. Thus Brandeis refused to concede self-evident legitimacy to legislative majorities for the same underlying reasons that he excoriated corporate America—because his moral touchstone was the individual standing alone. He implicitly understood, though he never adequately articulated, the tenuousness of a conception of society built from this premise, because the individual for Brandeis always stood outside social life, was always homeless.

Brandeis thus accepted the premise that Hannah Arendt has identified as the fundamental social reality for European Jews. But Brandeis's example offers a significant emendation to Arendt's postulate that a homeless Jew can only see himself as pariah or parvenu. Brandeis tried, though without explicit acknowledgment, to carve a different social space for himself that confounded the distinction between insider and outsider. He did not thereby attempt to become an insider. Nor did he accept the continued existence of the social status of outsider, as a thoroughgoing pariah would do. Brandeis implicitly sought instead to dissolve the distinction. When Brandeis saw an outsider as such, he would strive to interpret this outsider's needs and concerns to the insiders of the day, to dissolve social boundaries by inspiring sympathy and fellow feeling on both sides. His role was not to speak as a pariah, though he often was heard as such; it was to stand at the boundary of insider status and work toward its dissolution.

This was not Felix Frankfurter's way. Insofar as he saw himself as a judge standing at the boundary between insider and outsider, his role conception was as persistent guardian of the demarcation. For Frankfurter and the generation of judges that followed Brandeis, the context of Brandeis's central social concern—conflict between capital and labor—did not seem to demand the same urgent attention. With the New Deal's recognition of labor's organizational rights and its entrenched political power, economic class distinctions no longer seemed salient depictions of insider/outsider status in American society. The impulses toward this demarcation did not, however, disappear; they changed focus.

Frankfurter accepted, even celebrated, these demarcations. He comprehended organized society as necessarily dependent on including some by excluding others. By the time of Earl Warren's appointment in 1953, however, a Court majority rejected this conception and embraced Brandeis's mission, as Frankfurter would not do.

The harbinger of this result, and the underlying ideological forces that pushed it forward, can be seen on the Court in the 1940s, in the dispute between Frankfurter and Hugo Black about exclusive reliance on constitutional text as opposed to invocation of supratextual "judicial conscience."[9] The dispute arose from a premise that both men shared—the premise that judicial authority depends for its legitimacy on its clear differentiation from the judge's "merely personal" views, that a judge must stand for, and stand within, some transcendent, authoritative social entity.

Frankfurter and Black each fiercely attacked the other for his failure to achieve this ideal: Frankfurter claiming, plausibly enough, that the constitutional texts on which Black relied did not yield the univocal commands that Black read into them, and that his "textualism" was thus a mask for the imposition of personal views;[10] and Black claiming, also plausibly enough, that Frankfurter's invocation of his "judicial conscience" was an open invitation for a judge to confound his authoritative impositions with his personal proclivities.[11] Neither man's position could achieve the goal that both men pursued; that goal was not attainable, and the fact of that unattainability pressed harder on Frankfurter, Black, and their contemporaries than on previous generations of judges.

Justice Rufus Peckham, for example, could write for the majority in *Lochner* that the state statute was "an unreasonable, unnecessary and arbitrary interference with the right of an individual to his personal liberty"[12] without visible embarrassment at the emptiness and consequent subjectivity of those evaluative standards. Peckham claimed that the content for those standards came from the normative premises that he shared with those who properly ruled American society. Peckham in effect portrayed himself nestled inside a shared subjectivity that linked him comfortably with all "who counted" for anything worthwhile. This shared subjectivity was hardly unanimous; Holmes saw it as such and disdained it as wholly arbitrary and therefore unworthy of allegiance. But Peckham did not pretend that this cultural centerpoint for which he spoke was universally shared; its very purpose was its non-universality, its comfortable, self-evident-seeming demarcation of an inside and an outside.

The social factors that sustained this sense of comfort among Peckham and his brethren were strained and strenuously challenged at the time, as I have indicated. The forces of social fragmentation apparent at the beginning of the twentieth century had become even more visible by its midpoint. Peckham's smug claims to insider status no longer offered the same comfort to Frankfurter, Black, and their contemporaries.

One small, but nonetheless revealing, reflection in judicial behavior of this greater social fragmentation was a subtly changed style of opinion-writing between Peckham's time and the modern Court. Justice Frankfurter charted the way in the unusual length of, and extensive reliance on citation of past precedents in, his opinions.[13] By our own era, following the social disorder of the 1960s, this Frankfurterian mode—the heavily footnoted, scholarly-seeming production—has become almost an obsession among the justices, as their opinions have occupied exponentially increasing numbers of pages in the United States Reports.[14]

Brandeis's opinions were correctly assessed as uncommonly lengthy documents for his time; as noted, their greater bulk was largely the result of his extensive recitation of the factual background of the dispute at issue intended to enlarge his colleagues' range of vision to include facts and perspectives outside their ordinary experience. Brandeis's colleagues could comfortably write short opinions, citing a few facts, a few prior precedents, and a few abstract propositions; Holmes was indeed the quickest of them all because, for all his skeptical relativism, he was quite complacent about social authority (and about his role in wielding that authority) on the premise that one end is as good as any other.[15] Frankfurter and his successors on the Court could not escape a greater sense of discomfort in the exercise of social authority than had been felt even by Brandeis and Holmes, much less by their more conventional colleagues. Thus the increased length of judicial opinions—much greater in bulk than Brandeis's productions—was directed toward a different purpose than Brandeis intended. The new length, and its increased reliance on past precedent of varying persuasiveness, was to bolster the legitimacy of judicial authority, not for Brandeis's purpose of altering the conventional conception of legitimate social authority.[16]

Contemporary judges talk so much more than their predecessors about the sources of their authority because they can no longer rely on unspoken understandings, on shared meanings that go deeper than words can convey. They are garrulous in order to reason, argue, charm, cajole—to talk themselves into the center of social life in a way that would never occur to those who saw themselves as immovably at this center. (This volubility, this profusion of words, was Frankfurter's way not only as a judge but as a Harvard law professor and, earlier, as a man on the make.) In whatever social setting, in the salon or in the courtroom, this is the mark of the parvenu.

These stylistic elements are not the only indications that judges generally now find themselves uncomfortably deprived of the customary insider's perspective. The more significant indications of this trait can be discerned in the substance of their decisions displaying a heightened sensitivity toward outsider status. This is the underlying meaning of the series of decisions from the 1930s addressing the status of blacks in the South that culminated in *Brown v. Board of Education*. The Supreme Court was in one sense, of course, merely responding to the successive litigative attacks skillfully mounted by the NAACP on all aspects of the racial subordination regime and to the background of increasing visibility and militancy among black civil rights advocates generally.[17] But the same litigative skills and threats of social turmoil had confronted the Court in the preceding generation regarding the interests and rights of workers; and the Court for the most part disregarded these claims.[18] Differential sensitivity to the social status of outsiders is the characteristic that best explains the differing judicial receptions of these successive litigative claimants.

The differing receptions cannot be explained by comparing the attitudes of the two generations of judges to judicial authority. *Brown* was the most ambitious invocation of judicial authority in this century, perhaps even in the Court's history, in its invalidation of a widespread, passionately espoused social practice blessed by the explicit constitutional sanction of the Court itself a half-century earlier. The audacious scope of *Brown* might not have troubled a Court confident of its own authority and prepared to rely on its own ipse dixit as the warrant for that authority—the Court that had decided *Lochner,* for example. But this was emphatically not the same Court that decided *Brown*. A majority of the *Brown* Court had come to the bench, appointed by Franklin Roosevelt, with the explicit agenda of ending the regime of rule by judiciary that *Lochner* symbolized.[19]

In retrospect, some have argued that the Roosevelt Court's repudiation of *Lochner* rejected only judicial intervention in economic regulation and not judicial activism to protect "personal rights."[20] This is a distinction, however, that would have made no sense to the justices who decided *Lochner:* they conceived themselves as invalidating an economic regulation in order to protect the personal rights of employer and employee to autonomy, to free choice in setting the terms of their relationship.[21] The imagined distinction between economic interests and personal rights was not the fulcrum that moved the Roosevelt Court to invalidate the race segregation regime.

Brown did indeed repudiate *Lochner*—not in the *Lochner* Court's assertion of judicial authority as such, but in its claim regarding social authority generally. The *Lochner* Court's vision of judicial and general social authority rested on the same premise: that some people owned this society (judges, employers, the "better sorts"), while others were mere "tenants at will," whose occasional privileges were held only on the sufferance of, and revocable at the unreviewable discretion of, the true owners. This confidence in the existence and legitimacy of a demarcation between social insiders and outsiders had profoundly eroded in the social experience of the judges who decided *Brown v. Board of Education*. The cruelties inflicted by insiders had become visible as a repressive attempt to maintain the apparent solidity of their brittle privileged status.

It was the smugness and unacknowledged cruelty, the barely masked repressive violence, in the maintenance of insider/outsider distinctions that *Lochner* and the regime of Southern racial subordination both epitomized. From this perspective, *Plessy v. Ferguson*[22] reflected the same conception of social authority as *Lochner.* (The *Lochner* majority was in fact composed wholly of justices who had decided *Plessy* nine years earlier; Justice Edward Douglass White alone changed position in the two cases; John Marshall Harlan dissented in both, and the two added *Lochner* dissenters, Oliver Wendell Holmes and William Day, had only recently joined the Court.) *Brown v. Board of Education* thus rejected both *Plessy* and *Lochner* at the same time and for the same reason: to repudiate the pattern of social authority based on the rigid imposition of insider/outsider status.

This was not the meaning of *Brown,* however, for every justice who concurred in that decision. Felix Frankfurter saw *Brown* as expanding the definition of social insiders, but not as casting any doubt either on the definitional enterprise itself or on the propriety of judges as officers presiding over this enterprise. Frankfurter's understanding of *Brown* was most noticeably revealed in his role as principal proponent within the Court of delay in implementing desegregation, through the "all deliberate speed" formula of *Brown II.*[23]

This delayed implementation can be justified as a device to eschew judicial authoritarianism and thereby to promote a Brandeisian process of "patient, careful argument [and] willingness to listen and to consider" among the Southern black and white adversaries and within majoritarian institutions.[24] From Alexander Bickel's eyewitness account of the internal Court deliberations at the time of *Brown,* it appears that Justice Robert Jackson in particular was responsive to these concerns.[25] But Frankfurter's embrace of delay and a correspondingly low enforcement profile by the Court appeared much more motivated by a wish to safeguard the Court's authority rather than to promote the authority of others. Thus, Bickel recounts,

> the perceptive listener . . . would have heard Mr. Justice Frankfurter probe the enforcement problem, worry

> about the possible gerrymandering of school districts that were supposedly not constituted on racial lines, and finally say: "Nothing could be worse from my point of view than for this Court to make an abstract declaration that segregation is bad and then have it evaded by tricks."[26]

"Nothing could be worse," as I read his point of view, because the Court's authority would be impeached, most likely with success because of the unpopularity of its decision. Frankfurter amplified this same concern in a letter to Justice Harlan five years later, when *Cooper v. Aaron* was pending before the Court. The "transcending issue," he said, was preserving "the Supreme Court as the authoritative organ of what the Constitution requires."[27]

The Court persisted in its cautious strategy regarding the implementation of *Brown* throughout Frankfurter's tenure.[28] When he retired from the Court in 1962, the increased militance of the Civil Rights movement and its more direct assault on conventional conceptions of social authority had not yet clearly come to the Court's attention. When cases presenting this militant challenge did come a few years later, the Warren Court's previous carefully knit unanimity in support of black civil rights unraveled. Those justices whose civil rights sympathies were undermined by their distaste for this increased militance explicitly drew on Frankfurter's decisions to buttress their claims to authority[29]—a reliance, I believe, in which Frankfurter himself would have concurred.

The increased black militance of the mid sixties essentially rejected the assimilationist demand that the social category of "insider" be opened to admit some (properly qualified) blacks—a demand Frankfurter was prepared to accept. The new militance bitterly criticized as inherently repressive the very idea of a centrist insider status, of a uniform preferred social identity at the summit of the assimilationist ambition.[30] To Frankfurter, this critique would have been anathema.[31]

Though these battle lines were not clearly drawn in the race relations cases during Frankfurter's tenure, one particular case in which he participated did directly address this underlying issue regarding the propriety and necessity of uniform delineations between insider and outsider status. The case was *Trop v. Dulles,*[32] decided in 1958, where the Court addressed a congressional act that removed citizenship status from any member of the armed forces convicted of desertion during wartime. The Court sharply divided in this case, revealing the ideological fault lines that would later shatter the reign of unanimity in race relations. A bare Court majority invalidated the act on the grounds that the "use of denationalization as a punishment" was inherently "cruel and unusual" and thus barred by the Eighth Amendment.[33] Chief Justice Warren explained for himself and Justices Black, Douglas, and Charles Whittaker:

> There may be involved no physical mistreatment, no primitive torture. There is instead the total destruction of the individual's status in organized society. . . . His very existence is at the sufferance of the country in which he happens to find himself. While any one country may accord him some rights, and presumably as long as he remained in this country he would enjoy the limited rights of an alien, no country need do so because he is stateless. Furthermore, his enjoyment of even the limited rights of an alien might be subject to termination at any time by reason of deportation. In short, the expatriate has lost the right to have rights.[34]

Justice Brennan, in a separate concurrence, amplified these concerns:

> In its material forms no one can today judge the precise consequences of expatriation, for happily American law has had little experience with this status. . . . [The consequences] are unknown and unknowable . . . [but] may be severe. Expatriation, in this respect, constitutes an es-

> pecially demoralizing sanction. The uncertainty, and the consequent psychological hurt, . . . must accompany one who becomes an outcast in his own land.[35]

Frankfurter, joined by Justices Harold Burton, Tom Clark, and John M. Harlan, rejected the majority's conclusion on several grounds: first, that expatriation is not "'punishment' in any valid constitutional sense";[36] and second, that even if it were punishment, it is not "cruel" because of "the substantial rights and privileges" that any stateless person has as an alien resident in this country.[37] To Warren's concern about the tenuousness of these protections, Frankfurter replied,

> [An expatriate] need not be in constant fear lest some dire and unforeseen fate be imposed on him by arbitrary governmental action—certainly not "while this Court sits" [citing Holmes]. The multitudinous decisions of this Court protective of the rights of aliens bear weighty testimony. And the assumption that brutal treatment is the inevitable lot of denationalized persons found in other countries is a slender basis on which to strike down an Act of Congress otherwise amply sustainable.[38]

Frankfurter's basic reason for finding the act "amply sustainable" was this: "It is not for us to deny that Congress might reasonably have believed the morale and fighting efficiency of our troops would be impaired if our soldiers knew that their fellows who had abandoned them in their time of greatest need were to remain in the communion of our citizens."[39]

The Court majority valued the "communion of . . . citizens," in a sense, even more passionately than Frankfurter, because they were unwilling to accept the possibility that anyone might be forced to forfeit it. For the majority, the condition of "statelessness" held a special terror and thus warranted their virtually unprecedented invocation of the Eighth Amendment proscription of "cruel and unusual punishment." This outcast status had primarily an emotive and symbolic force for the majority justices. They explicitly acknowledged that the practical consequences of the status were unknown and possibly insubstantial. A fear deeper than practicalities moved them to their conclusion—the symbolism of "the total destruction of the individual's status in organized society" (in Warren's words),[40] the "psychological hurt, which must accompany one who becomes an outcast in his own land" (in Brennan's words).[41]

There is a resonance here, and particularly in Brennan's explicit invocation of the psychology of outcast status, that links *Trop* with the Court's opinion in *Brown* and the centrality of the "psychological hurt" of the social outcast status at stake there.[42] Recall this formulation in the *Brown* opinion, its only substantive criticism of racial segregation: "To separate [school children] from others of similar age and qualifications solely because of their race generates a feeling of inferiority as to their status in the community that may affect their hearts and minds in a way unlikely ever to be undone."[43]

This special sensitivity toward the outcast status of blacks thus evident in *Brown* was revealed as an intense revulsion against the status as such among a Court majority in *Trop*. This revulsion dominated the work of that majority in a wide range of subjects: thus the Warren Court's solicitude toward atheists[44] and communists,[45] toward criminal defendants[46] and convicted criminals,[47] toward illegitimate children.[48] In all of these matters, Frankfurter held back. Occasionally he would join with the majority to advance some increased protection for an "outcast" claimant; but never with the passion or the consistent concern for the outsider as such that gripped the Warren Court virtually throughout its tenure.

The Warren Court majority thus reiterated Brandeis's general stance; and there were also specific links to Brandeis's position in at least two matters. The first was the Warren Court's embrace of Brandeis's "retreat from the world . . .

[for] solitude and privacy" (and his somewhat romanticized vision of social alienation). In *Griswold v. Connecticut,*[49] the Court enshrined in the Constitution the "right to privacy" that Brandeis had espoused in dissent on the bench almost forty years earlier and in the *Harvard Law Review* some forty years before that.[50] (Frankfurter had retired before *Griswold* was decided; but he had turned away from the opportunity to reach this result in an earlier case.)[51]

The second link with Brandeis was less overt, but of more pervasive significance for the Warren Court majority. The link was in *Trop v. Dulles* itself. The Court majority not only excoriated state imposition of outcast status; it did so on the basis of a virtually explicit empathic identification with the oppressed status of European Jews—the same empathy that Brandeis himself extended in his Zionist involvement. Frankfurter, in his *Trop* dissent, dissociated himself from this position—again, almost explicitly.

None of this was openly avowed in *Trop,* but all of it seems to have been clearly understood as such by all of the justices writing in the case. The invocation of the European Jewish experience occurred in Chief Justice Warren's plurality opinion with the resounding proclamation, "In short, the expatriate has lost the right to have rights."[52] For all its rhetorical force, this makes little sense as a proposition of American constitutional law: the Fourteenth Amendment guarantees of due process and equal protection explicitly extend to "persons" as distinct from "citizens."

The chief justice was not, however, relying on American positive law in making this pronouncement. He was in fact relying on an analysis by Hannah Arendt of the German legal regime that led to the extermination of the Jews, though he did not cite her work as such. Arendt originated the phrase "a right to have rights" in her portrayal, in *The Origins of Totalitarianism,* of the legal significance of expatriation laws;[53] the phrase was reiterated in a student Comment in the *Yale Law*

Journal in 1955 ("[E]xpatriation represents a loss of the right to have rights—loss of membership in an organized community capable of guaranteeing any rights at all" [quoting Arendt]);[54] the student Comment was explicitly "incorporate[d] by reference" as a "masterful analysis" by Chief Judge Charles Clark in his dissenting opinion in the Second Circuit's disposition of *Trop;*[55] and Chief Justice Warren cited this portion of Clark's opinion, fully quoting it in a footnote,[56] in the first sentence of the paragraph that ended with the proclamation of the phrase itself.

The provenance of the phrase is thus clear, though unacknowledged by the chief justice. It is as if Warren were unwilling directly to draw the links that he saw between the challenged congressional act and the Nazi treatment of Jews—an understandable reluctance, since the parallel would not sit comfortably with the members of Congress who had voted for the expatriation measure. But the linkage was there in Warren's opinion nonetheless: partially hidden, encoded, but plainly there. Here is the paragraph from Arendt that appears on the same page in her book where the *Trop* phrase originated:

> The calamity of the rightless is not that they are deprived of life, liberty, and the pursuit of happiness, or of equality before the law and freedom of opinion—formulas which were designed to solve problems *within* given communities—but that they no longer belong to any community whatsoever. Their plight is not that they are not equal before the law, but that no law exists for them; not that they are oppressed but that nobody wants even to oppress them. Only in the last stage of a rather lengthy process is their right to live threatened; only if they remain perfectly "superfluous," if nobody can be found to "claim" them, may their lives be in danger. Even the Nazis started their extermination of Jews by first depriving them of all legal status (the status of second-class citizenship) and cutting them off from the

> world of the living by herding them into ghettos and concentration camps; and before they set the gas chambers into motion they had carefully tested the ground and found out to their satisfaction that no country would claim these people. The point is that a condition of complete rightlessness was created before the right to live was challenged.[57]

If the Court majority's reliance on Arendt's analysis and possible parallels between the American and Nazi expatriation statutes was hidden from the readers of its opinion, that reliance was nonetheless clear to Justice Frankfurter. He criticized this reliance thus: "the assumption that brutal treatment is the inevitable lot of denationalized persons found in other countries is a slender basis on which to strike down an Act of Congress."[58] Two points appear to be compressed here: that stateless status in other countries did not inevitably lead to "brutal treatment," and that, whatever occurred in "other countries," it cannot happen here (or at least, as Frankfurter observed two sentences earlier in his opinion, "not while this Court sits").

Frankfurter disregarded at least one earlier example in this country when "brutal treatment" had been inflicted on "denationalized persons." The example was black slavery; and the Supreme Court, far from providing protection, had been the direct instrument of expatriation by its holding in *Dred Scott* that no black person, whether slave or free, could ever become a citizen of the United States.[59] The Court majority in *Trop* did not cite *Dred Scott* to buttress its conclusion regarding the inherent brutality of expatriation. The American treatment of blacks did, however, provide a normative framework for the Court majority. The majority's reasoning in *Trop* rested not only on rejection of involuntary expatriation as such but on revulsion against any forced imposition of outcast status.

The American slave regime rested not simply on black expatriation but more fundamentally on a system of caste subordination. After the formal abolition of slavery, this caste system was resurrected in Jim Crow, which the Supreme Court approved in *Plessy v. Ferguson*. Justice Frankfurter joined, of course, in the Warren Court's decision overruling *Plessy*. Frankfurter's refusal to join the Court majority in *Trop* demonstrates, however, the limited character of the fault he found in *Plessy:* he rejected racial discrimination, but not the existence of a caste system as such. For the Warren Court majority, as it revealed in *Trop,* the evil of *Plessy* went beyond racism; a segregated black, like an expatriated soldier, was "an outcast in his own land." The Warren Court majority would not tolerate any imposition of outcast status as such.

Frankfurter did not agree. In his *Trop* dissent, he invoked Oliver Wendell Holmes to justify his refusal to condemn the congressional imposition of outcast status:

> The awesome power of this Court to invalidate [national] legislation . . . must be exercised with the utmost restraint. Mr. Justice Holmes, one of the profoundest thinkers who ever sat on this Court, expressed the conviction that "I do not think the United States would come to an end if we lost our power to declare an Act of Congress void. I do think the Union would be imperiled if we could not make that declaration as to the laws of the several States." He did not, of course, deny that the power existed to strike down congressional legislation, nor did he shrink from its exercise. But the whole of his work during his thirty years of service on this Court should be a constant reminder that the power to invalidate legislation must not be exercised as if . . . it stood as the sole bulwark against unwisdom or excesses of the moment.[60]

Frankfurter thus draped himself in the Brahmin's robes and revealed that he, like Holmes, was prepared to see himself as the obedient instrument of national power.[61] If he might occasionally subject national legislation to critical scrutiny, it was only because the received authoritative constitutional tradition itself gave this role to judges, and not because this role reflected a deep-rooted social imperative demanding an independent—that is to say, alienated, outcast—perspective on all exercise of authoritative power. If Frankfurter had grasped this perspective, he would have seen what the Warren Court majority saw in *Trop v. Dulles:* the ominous connections between forced expatriation laws and the Nazi extermination policy, the parallels between expatriation, the Nazis, and the American racial caste regime. Frankfurter, however, saw none of this; or if he saw it, he turned away.

There was an earlier occasion, an unofficial occasion, when Frankfurter also refused to give credence to disturbing possibilities regarding Nazi policies. This was in 1942, when a member of the Polish underground, Jan Karski, secretly came to Washington and the ambassador of the Polish government in exile arranged a meeting with Frankfurter. Karski, according to his subsequent account, described Nazi genocide in the concentration camps. Frankfurter responded, "A man like me talking to a man like you must be totally honest. So I am. So I say: I do not believe you." The Polish ambassador rejoined, "Felix, how can you say such a thing? You know he is saying the truth. He was checked and rechecked in London and here. Felix, what are you saying?" Frankfurter answered, "I did not say that he's lying. I said that I don't believe him. There is a difference. My mind, my heart they are made in such a way that I cannot conceive it."[62]

6

Priests and Prophets

The Brandeisian perspective remained dominant in the work of the Warren Court until 1967. One decision in that year marked the end. This case had originated four years earlier when, on Good Friday and again on Easter Sunday, Martin Luther King, Jr., had led protest marches through Birmingham, Alabama. The day before the first march, city officials had served Dr. King and his followers with an *ex parte* injunction they had obtained from a state court that forbade any massed gatherings unless the demonstrators first obtained a parade permit from the city. That same day, King had announced his intention to conduct the demonstrations notwithstanding the injunction:

> We are now confronted with recalcitrant forces in the Deep South that will use the courts to perpetuate the unjust and illegal system of racial separation. . . . This is raw tyranny under the guise of maintaining law and order. We cannot in all good conscience obey such an injunction. . . . We do this not out of any disrespect for the law but out of the highest respect for *the* law. This is not an attempt to evade or defy the law or engage in chaotic anarchy. Just as in all good conscience we cannot obey unjust laws, neither can we respect the unjust use of the courts.[1]

On the day after Easter, the state court found King and the other demonstration leaders in contempt and imposed five-day jail sentences on them. The court refused to consider any challenge to the constitutionality either of its earlier injunction or of the city parade permit ordinance on which the injunction had been based.

In 1967 the Supreme Court upheld these convictions. In retrospect this decision, *Walker v. City of Birmingham,*[2] marked the beginning of the end of the Warren Court era's embrace of the pariah perspective. This was not only because the Court approved the imprisonment of King, who at that time was the embodiment of the prophetic outcast for American society. More significantly, it was because of the basis on which the Court approved his imprisonment. King had announced his intention to follow his independent conscience rather than to obey an unjust law or judicial order. The Court held that even if the state judge's order were unjust, King was nonetheless bound to obey it. He could obtain release from this obligation only by appealing to other judges (and ultimately to the Supreme Court justices), who alone were authorized to countermand, because they alone were hierarchically superior to, the Alabama trial judge. So the Supreme Court held in an opinion by Justice Potter Stewart joined by four others (Justices Black, Clark, Harlan, and White).

In reaching this conclusion, the Court relied on the same reasoning that Frankfurter had set out in his separate opinion in *United Mine Workers,* arguing that the union was obliged to obey a court order notwithstanding its illegality until a higher court had so ruled. Recall Frankfurter's rhetoric: "The Founders knew that Law alone saves a society from being rent by internecine strife or ruled by mere brute power. . . . To that end, they set apart a body of men, who were to be the depositories of law."[3] This same confounding of the law and the judges was at the heart of the Court's ruling in the *City of Birmingham* case, as the last words of its opinion revealed:

> In the fair administration of justice no man can be judge in his own case, however exalted his station, however righteous his motives, and irrespective of his race, color, politics, or religion. This Court cannot hold that the petitioners were constitutionally free to ignore all the procedures of the law and carry their battle to the streets. One may sympathize with the petitioners' impatient commitment to their cause. But respect for judicial process is a small price to pay for the civilizing hand of law, which alone can give abiding meaning to constitutional freedom.[4]

King thus failed to pay homage to the constituted hierarchy of judicial authority by acting on his own judgment rather than testing the legality of the injunction through (and visibly submitting himself to) the regular judicial process. This, the Supreme Court held, was imprisonable contempt.

The Court's charge that King claimed to "be judge in his own case" distorted the true issue at stake. King was not asserting absolute immunity from social sanctions or from judicial imposition of such sanctions for his conduct of the demonstration. He claimed only that if the initial injunction had been unconstitutionally imposed, then his disregard for that injunction should not be punishable; if, however, the Supreme Court ultimately concluded that the state judge had lawful authority to impose the injunction, then King conceded that he should be punished.[5] It was the Court, not King, who relied on the rule of "mere brute power" in demanding unquestioning obedience to an unlawful judicial order. Their formulation was a variant of the old cliché for Wild West vigilante justice: not "shoot first," but its close cousin "obey first," and ask questions later.

When Frankfurter had taken the same position in his separate opinion in *United Mine Workers,* a personal motivation might plausibly have been discerned for his stance—a prideful demand for deference to his superior social status as judge, an unwillingness to acknowledge that anyone might properly question the pedigree, the legality, of his or any of his brother judges' status or actions—and beneath this high-handedness, an insecurity about the legitimacy of his claim to superior status that made him unwilling to accept any overt challenge to it. No similar suspicions about unique personal motivation leap from the biographies of Justice Stewart or the four others who joined him in the *City of Birmingham* majority. There is nonetheless a functionally equivalent uncertainty about the solidity of his social status that can be glimpsed in Stewart's opinion—an uncertainty that, unlike Frankfurter's special source of personal insecurity, was widely shared among judges at the time, who found themselves confronted by unaccustomed challenges to their claims, and all claims, to social authority.

This uncertainty was revealed in the concluding paragraph of Stewart's opinion, where he refused, as he put it, to hold that the demonstrators "were free to ignore all the procedures of the law and carry their battle to the streets."[6] Justice Brennan amplified the significance of this observation at the end of his dissenting opinion (joined by Chief Justice Warren and Justices Douglas and Fortas):

> We cannot permit fears of "riots" and "civil disobedience" generated by slogans like "Black Power" to divert our attention from what is here at stake—not violence or the right of the State to control its streets and sidewalks, but the insulation from attack of *ex parte* orders and legislation upon which they are based even when patently impermissible prior restraints on the exercise of First Amendment rights.[7]

In Brennan's comment, one can hear echoes of conference room and corridor conversations among the justices: informal revelations of underlying fears about the widespread urban race riots of the mid 1960s and popular resistance to the Vietnam War, which had become visibly insistent by 1967. No matter that this social turmoil (this "internecine strife," as Frankfurter would put it) was by then more focused in racial conflict in Northern urban areas (and in intergenerational conflict on college campuses) than in the Southern setting of King's civil rights protests in 1963 when the case itself arose.

King himself had struggled to contain these more explosive challenges by blacks to constituted white authority, with markedly decreased success, between 1963 and 1967.[8] When the justices deliberated their response to King's earlier challenge to the unjust exercise of judicial authority, they could not avoid viewing that challenge in the context of these later events. By a narrow margin of one vote on the Court, the parvenu perspective prevailed—the perspective more fearful of challenges to constituted social authority, less confident that their social status (or anyone's) within that conventional hierarchy would receive widespread unforced acknowledgement and deference.

1967 was only the beginning. King's assassination the next year loosed an eruption of racial violence that amplified these fearful implications. Nixon's election to the presidency that same year and his appointment in quick succession of four members of the Court—Chief Justice Warren Burger and Justices Harry Blackmun, Lewis Powell, and William Rehnquist—were instrumental in securing the dominance of the parvenu perspective on the Supreme Court that persists to this day.

One question of recurrent, even obsessive, concern to the Court since 1967 has most clearly revealed the contemporary triumph of this perspective. That question has been the constitutional status of the death penalty. In his opinion in *Trop v. Dulles,* on his way toward condemning expatriation, Chief Justice Warren explicitly conceded the constitutionality of capital punishment, but argued nonetheless that this was not a "license to the Government to devise any [imaginable] punishment short of death."[9] Barely a decade later, in 1968, a Court majority for the first time acknowledged substantial doubts about the death penalty. Holding that states might not exclude from capital cases all jurors with "conscientious scruples" against the death penalty, the Court observed that such a jury, "culled of all who harbor doubts about the wisdom of capital punishment, . . . can speak only for a distinct and dwindling minority."[10] The Court then added a footnote seeming to endorse this quoted observation from a well-known abolitionist:

> The division [between supporters and opponents of the death penalty] is not between rich and poor, highbrow and lowbrow, Christians and atheists; it is between those who have charity and those who have not. . . . The test of one's humanity is whether one is able to accept this fact—not as lip service, but with the shuddering recognition of a kinship: here but for the grace of God, drop I.[11]

This invocation of an empathic identification with the outcast was a clear statement of the theme that had dominated the work of the Warren Court majority. The link between this statement and *Brown v. Board of Education* was evident not only in the fact that blacks appeared disproportionately subjected to capital punishment (and that the Southern states were the most prolific dispensers of this penalty) but also because the NAACP Legal Defense Fund, which had led the litigative campaign against race segregation, had decided in 1963 to make abolition of the death penalty a central litigative goal.[12] Just as the Court had moved from *Brown*'s repudiation of the outcast status of blacks to *Trop*'s revulsion at that status itself in the expatriation law, so now the Court, pressed by the NAACP, edged toward condemnation of state executions, this most visible official infliction of outcast status.

By the end of Warren's tenure, the Court was not prepared to address the constitutional validity of the death penalty frontally. Its decision in the jury exclusion case was an unmistakable signal of the Court majority's concern, but not much more than that, even in its immediate practical impact on the administration of the penalty.[13] Just four years later, however, in 1972, the five remaining members of the Warren Court joined together, against the united opposition of the new Nixon appointees, to invalidate all existing state death penalty statutes. This decision, in *Furman v. Georgia*,[14] can be seen in retrospect as the last gasp of the Warren Court majority's concern for outcast status, for the Brandeisian project of confounding social distinctions between insider and outsider.

The five justices who voted together in *Furman* did not constitute the Warren Court majority that had invariably shared this concern. Only three were the surviving remnant of that majority: Justices William O. Douglas, William Brennan, and Thurgood Marshall (who, though he joined the Warren Court only at its end in 1967, had been the principal advocate for this perspective before the Court as the chief counsel of the NAACP Legal Defense Fund). These survivors concluded that the death penalty violated the constitutional injunction against cruel and unusual punishments. Justice Brennan's separate opinion was most explicit in educing this conclusion from the Warren era's concern for the outcast; he did so by elaborating on implications of Hannah Arendt's phrase, used in *Trop*, that expatriation was invalid because it imposed loss of "the right to have rights":

> The calculated killing of a human being by the State involves, by its very nature, a denial of the executed person's humanity. The contrast with the plight of a person punished by imprisonment is evident. An individual in prison does not lose "the right to have rights." . . . A prisoner remains a member of the human family. . . . His punishment is not irrevocable. . . . [Y]et the finality of death precludes relief. An executed person has indeed "lost the right to have rights." As one 19th century proponent of punishing criminals by death declared, "When

> a man is hung, there is an end of our relations with him. His execution is a way of saying, 'You are not fit for this world, take your chance elsewhere.'"[15]

The two other remaining Warren Court members—Justices Potter Stewart and Byron White—had not shared this same unvarying revulsion at outcast status; they were occasionally uneasy about this status, but less consistent and, one might say, more agnostic in their concern. Their uneasiness at the official imposition of this status was clear, however, in their separate rationales in *Furman* for invalidating the extant death penalty statutes. Stewart expressed this uneasiness most vividly in his observation that "these death sentences are cruel and unusual in the same way that being struck by lightning is cruel and unusual."[16] By this he meant that the death penalty fell on "a capriciously selected random handful"; it was "so wantonly and so freakishly imposed."[17] Capital punishment was not inherently invalid for Stewart or for White, just as the status of social outcast was not invariably offensive for them. The constitutional offense for Stewart, as for White, was the apparent irrationality of the differentiation between those punished by prison terms and those executed, between those who remained inside and those irrevocably extruded from communal life.

Four years later the Supreme Court once again considered the constitutionality of capital punishment. In the interim, thirty-five states had re-enacted death penalty statutes (in different formats as each state variously tried to comply with the strictures of *Furman*). This time a Court majority validated some of these statutes and thus approved capital punishment in principle.[18] Only Justices Brennan and Marshall remained adamant in opposing all forms of the death penalty. (These two by then were the last survivors of the Warren Court majority; Douglas had been replaced by John Paul Stevens.)

Justice White was now prepared to validate all of the new statutes, while Stewart approved some but not others. For our purposes, the differences between them are not significant; the important proposition is that neither man was prepared to stand firm against the imposition of outcast status that capital punishment in any format necessarily represents. The shift in Stewart's position is more illuminating than White's, not only because Stewart's successive opinions more clearly reveal his thinking than do White's, but more significantly because Stewart had been much more openly uncomfortable with capital punishment even before *Furman*. Most notably, Stewart had voted with the Warren Court majority in the 1968 capital jury exclusion case, while White had dissented; indeed, Stewart had written the Court's opinion in that case, and it was thus under his signature that death penalty advocates were apparently certified as lacking "charity," as failing a critical "test of one's humanity."[19]

What eroded Stewart's sympathy as a justice for these outcasts from 1968, when he appeared "able to accept . . . the shuddering recognition of a kinship," to 1972, when he appeared to act on this kinship by ruling that those condemned to death were rationally indistinguishable from those permitted to remain alive, to 1976, when he was willing to accept the executions of some? In his visible forfeiture of sympathy, Justice Stewart epitomized the shift from the Warren Court majority's almost invariable revulsion at official impositions of outcast status to the Burger Court majority's almost invariable approbation. What changed for Stewart?

One obvious change between 1968 and 1976 was an apparent shift in public opinion—a shift that Stewart explicitly noted in his successive opinions. In 1968 he observed that the proponents of capital punishment were "a distinct and dwindling minority."[20] In 1976, faced with the re-enactment of death penalty statutes by a majority of states, Stewart recanted: "[D]evelopments during the four years since *Furman* . . .

[make it] evident that a large proportion of American society continues to regard [capital punishment] as an appropriate and necessary criminal sanction."[21] Perhaps this is the whole explanation for Stewart's change of heart: the Supreme Court "follows th' iliction returns," as Mr. Dooley observed. I believe, however, that more than this moved Stewart. Popular sentiment was relevant to him, not because he felt obliged (like an elected official) to follow it, but because as a justice he feared the social consequences of this sentiment.

Stewart identified these consequences in his 1976 opinion: "In part, capital punishment is an expression of society's moral outrage at particularly offensive conduct. This function may be unappealing to many, but it is essential in an ordered society that asks its citizens to rely on legal processes rather than self-help to vindicate their wrongs."[22] Stewart then reiterated an observation that he had originally made in his *Furman* opinion:

> The instinct for retribution is part of the nature of man, and channeling that instinct in the administration of criminal justice serves an important purpose in promoting the stability of a society governed by law. When people begin to believe that organized society is unwilling or unable to impose upon criminal offenders the punishment they "deserve," then there are sown the seeds of anarchy—of self-help, vigilante justice, and lynch law.[23]

This concern about "channeling" social conflict into stabilizing legal institutions to avert anarchic popular impulses toward "self-help" is the same rationale Stewart articulated for imprisoning Dr. King and his followers in *Walker v. City of Birmingham.* They too had engaged in "self-help," they had "ignore[d] all the procedures of the law and carr[ied] their battle to the streets."[24] From the same factual predicate that American society was gripped by overt conflict—between blacks and whites or between criminal offenders and those who demanded their execution—Stewart drew the same conclusion: that formal institutions must suppress popular expression of hostilities.[25] If this suppression entailed perpetuation of a degraded outcast class, as in the case of Martin Luther King, Jr., or the creation of an outcast class, as in public executions, this was regrettable, but nonetheless a "small price to pay for the civilizing hand of law," to avert "anarchy."[26]

This was the basis on which Stewart's sympathies for outcasts were forfeited. He accordingly joined forces with other justices who had been less concerned than he about the maintenance of outcast status, who had indeed more consistently been prepared—like Justice Frankfurter throughout his judicial career—to regard the maintenance of distinctly bounded outcast classes as intrinsically justified, as the very definition of ordered social life.

Stewart's position carries a special irony. The times of most openly explosive social turmoil have also been the times when the most virulent oppression has been inflicted with escalating intensity on outcast groups. The terrible crescendo of European anti-Semitism in the Nazi regime was surely linked, as Arendt saw, to the social upheavals in the Germany of the 1930s.[27] Justice Brandeis drew this same lesson from American experience:

> Those who won our independence by revolution were not cowards. They did not exalt order at the cost of liberty. They recognized the risks to which all human institutions are subject. But they knew that order cannot be secured merely through fear of punishment or its infraction; . . . that fear breeds repression; that repression breeds hate; that hate menaces stable government.[28]

Brandeis wrote this in *Whitney v. California* in the course of arguing, against the Court majority, that a state statute forbidding organized advocacy of "criminal syndicalism" violated the free speech and assembly guarantees of the First Amendment.[29] Brandeis's position illuminates the basic characteristics of those who are capable of active, sustained sympathy for outsiders.

The statute at issue in *Whitney v. California* was enacted in 1919 in the wake of the Russian Revolution and at the height of the "Red Scare" in this country; it was used by California to secure convictions of the organizers of the Communist Labor party of that state. The social conflict reflected in this case was as openly waged and as raw as the racial conflict that surrounded King's conviction in the 1960s and more plausibly anarchic in its impact than the conflicts between outraged lynch mobs and criminal offenders that Justice Stewart feverishly imagined in the 1970s.

Brandeis was not deflected by fears of turmoil from his solicitude for outcasts as such. He explicitly invoked this concern in his *Whitney* opinion: "Men feared witches and burned women. It is the function of speech to free men from the bondage of irrational fears."[30] The constitutional role of a judge, as he saw it, was to interrupt the escalating cycle of fear, repression, and hatred that maintenance of an outcast status entailed—not, to extend the application of his concern, to contribute to this escalating impulse as in the *City of Birmingham* decision or to acquiesce in it as in the more recent death penalty decisions.

Brandeis's tolerance for openly waged social conflict did not, however, come easily for him. His distaste for such conflict—for "self-help," as Stewart phrased it, whether by insiders or outsiders—was most vividly expressed in a dissenting opinion he wrote in 1921. In the *Duplex Printing Press* case,[31] the Court ruled that Congress's enactment of the Clayton Act of 1914, restricting federal court authority to issue injunctions in labor disputes, did not apply to "secondary boycotts" that violated state common law. Brandeis objected that such boycotts did not violate common law norms, and that in the

Clayton Act Congress "declared that the relations between employers of labor and workingmen were competitive relations, that organized competition was not harmful and that [such competition] justified injuries necessarily inflicted in its course."[32] Though Brandeis acceded to this congressional intention, as he read it, he was not enthusiastic. He ended his dissent thus.

> Because I have come to the conclusion that both the common law of a state and a statute of the United States declare the right of industrial combatants to push their struggle to the limits of the justification of self-interest, I do not wish to be understood as attaching any constitutional or moral sanction to that right. All rights are derived from the purposes of the society in which they exist; above all rights rises duty to the community. The conditions developed in industry may be such that those engaged in it cannot continue their struggle without danger to the community. But it is not for judges to determine whether such conditions exist, nor is it their function to set the limits of permissible contest and to declare the duties which the new situation demands. This is the function of the legislature which, while limiting individual and group rights of aggression and defense, may substitute processes of justice for the more primitive method of trial by combat.[33]

Brandeis is not prescribing here an unvarying deference by judges to majoritarian legislative institutions—unlike Holmes then or Frankfurter later. Brandeis's position must be understood in the context of his general attitude toward labor conflict in his time, and the reflexive stance that judges had been taking to protect employers' maintenance of their prerogatives, their insider status, against the claims of employees. In the Clayton Act, organized labor had enlisted congressional support to limit these judicial interventions—a limitation to which the Court majority gave short shrift in *Duplex Printing Press*. If Congress had aggravated employees' aggrieved outsider status by imposing additional burdens of subordination on them, it is not clear that Brandeis would have counseled deference. His condemnation of the criminal syndicalism statute in *Whitney v. California* suggests the contrary.

Brandeis's basic goal in these cases, as in his prior role as the "people's attorney," was to work toward a resolution of social conflict that would transcend the terms of that conflict, that would render irrelevant the contending parties' self-conceptions as insiders or outsiders. It was for this reason that Brandeis was willing to tolerate openly waged social conflict and to enjoin that toleration on those who wielded state coercive authority in other institutional settings. In effect, he struck a strategic alliance with outcasts in order to serve his longer-range social ameliorative purposes. His goal was to resolve social conflict, not to foment it. He was troubled by the violence involved in this conflict, but he was nonetheless convinced that imposed order would not yield social peace if that order merely ratified the existing, chafing differentiations between insider and outsider.

The foundation for Brandeis's persistently reiterated position was his unwavering empathic identification with those in outcast status. When he wrote in his *Duplex Printing Press* dissent of the "danger to the community" from unrestrained labor violence, he was simultaneously preparing his draft dissent in the *Coronado Coal Company* case sympathetically portraying the bases for the violent conduct of the striking and dismissed union workers, whose "standard of living" was under assault by the mining companies and was not considered "property" worthy of protection by established legal institutions.[34] Though Brandeis explicitly condemned the workers' violence in the *Coronado* case, their conduct did not forfeit his sympathy with their rage and frustration or override his conviction that a coercive response to their violence that merely ratified the imposition of outcast status on them would ultimately breed more destructive violence.

Brandeis thus persisted in his sympathy for outsiders, notwithstanding either the provocations of their disruptive conduct or the opportunities offered by his own social attainments for Brandeis to define himself as an insider. What might account for this persistence? Not his Jewishness as such; this element of his background could have driven him to seize the possibilities for abandoning outsider status, as Frankfurter's career suggests, as much as to cherish such status. But Brandeis's sense of his own Jewishness nonetheless provides a way to understand the depth of his commitment to outcasts. It is the meaning that Brandeis forged from Judaism, not the sole meaning that inevitably would arise for any American Jew, that holds the key.

Recall that Brandeis acknowledged no strong affiliation with Judaism until he was in his mid fifties, and that the bond that drew him then was Zionism rather than religious Judaism. The moment of Brandeis's mid-life conversion, as it were, to Zionism can be identified with some precision. It came in August 1912, as Brandeis related in a 1940 conversation with his biographer, Alpheus Thomas Mason.[35] In that month, Jacob De Haas, an editor of a Boston Jewish newspaper, came to see Brandeis at his Cape Cod summer home to discuss funding for Woodrow Wilson's presidential campaign. Brandeis had briefly met De Haas two years earlier, but did not know that De Haas had been a close associate of Theodore Herzl's and had been dispatched by him to America several years earlier with a mission to foster the establishment of American Zionism.

On Cape Cod, when their political discussion had ended, Brandeis escorted De Haas to the railway station. As they walked together, according to Brandeis's recollection, De Haas asked Brandeis if he were related to Lewis Dembitz. Brandeis said, yes, Dembitz was his maternal uncle, and asked why De

Haas inquired. De Haas answered that Dembitz (who had died five years earlier) was "a noble Jew" and described to Brandeis both his uncle's involvement in Zionism and the movement itself.[36] Brandeis, as Mason recounted, "was so profoundly aroused that he forgot vacation plans and invited his caller to stay for lunch and take a later train."[37] From that moment, Brandeis's passion for Zionism was fired. De Haas stayed that day for two hours, at Brandeis's request sent him extensive literature about the Zionist movement, was the instrument for Brandeis's rapid ascension to the leadership of American Zionism in 1914, and became Brandeis's most trusted adjutant in Zionist affairs thereafter.

De Haas did not exaggerate the importance of Brandeis's uncle in American Zionism or of Judaism in his uncle's life. Alone among all of Brandeis's relatives, Dembitz was a devoutly observant Jew.[38] He was also an attorney (again, alone among Brandeis's relatives), a scholar (who published, among other things, a study of Jewish ritual practice), a political activist (he gave one of the seconding speeches for Lincoln's nomination as a delegate to the 1860 Republican national convention and was an outspoken opponent of slavery in Kentucky, a slave state); and he was an early Zionist adherent.[39]

De Haas did not know—though one surmises from his later writings that he hoped, and perhaps even guessed, in his zeal to affiliate Brandeis with the Zionist cause[40]—that Brandeis had been devoted to, and profoundly influenced by, his uncle. When Louis was in his early teens, he changed his name to honor his uncle.[41] His given name at birth had been Louis David; he became Louis Dembitz Brandeis. His decision to become a lawyer was also decisively influenced by his uncle's example.[42] He did not then, or ever, follow his uncle's example in religious observance; but near the end of Brandeis's life, after he had retired from the Court, he described the aura that Dembitz's religiosity conveyed:

> In the home of my parents there was no Jewish Sabbath, nor in my own home. But I recall vividly the joy and awe with which my uncle, Lewis Dembitz, welcomed the arrival of the day and the piety with which he observed it. I remember the extra delicacies, lighting of the candles, prayers over a cup of wine, quaint chants, and Uncle Lewis poring over books most of the day. I remember more particularly an elusive something about him which was spoken of as the "Sabbath peace" and which years later brought to my mind a passage from Addison in which he speaks of stealing a day out of life to live. That elusive something prevailed in many a home in Boston on a Sunday and was not wanting at Harvard on the same day. Uncle Lewis used to say that he was enjoying a foretaste of heaven. I used to think, and do so now, that we need on earth the Jewish-Puritan Sabbath without its oppressive restrictions.[43]

The origins of Brandeis's attraction to Zionism can thus be plausibly traced to his uncle's example. There is more in Brandeis's devotion, however, than his simple homage to an admired relative. The special attractions of his uncle's Jewishness for Brandeis can be more fully grasped by considering the source of Lewis Dembitz's own religious devotion. Here too it is possible to identify with some precision the moment that this devotion appeared as a significant force in Dembitz's life. According to Brandeis's mother, in 1846 Lewis was living away from his family, enrolled in a school near Prague. By her account, Lewis, "then thirteen years old, left to himself, suddenly became an ardent orthodox Jew, unfortunately of such intensity of belief that it affected his whole life."[44]

Brandeis's mother, Frederika, gave this account as part of an extended series of letters she wrote to her son between 1880 and 1886. The occasion for these letters was Brandeis's request—frequently reiterated, according to the text of the letters themselves—that his mother record the experiences of her early childhood. By her account, the Dembitz family had not been in any way religiously observant.[45] The father was a physician educated in Prague who, to earn his somewhat tenuous livelihood, moved his family from one small Polish town to another until 1840, when Frederika was eleven and Lewis was seven. In that year two disasters struck the family in quick succession: the youngest child, Theodore, died in an accident, and a few months later their mother died. Frederika and Lewis were sent soon thereafter by their father to live with relatives in Prague.

The death of her mother was the one central event that virtually dominated Frederika's narrative account some forty years later to her son Louis. Frederika clearly saw the origins and ascribed the negative cast to her brother Lewis's later intense embrace of Judaism in the impact of their mother's death: "No child," she wrote, "has ever felt the loss of his mother more than Ludwig [Lewis] did. She had had a most wholesome influence on him and his whole life would have been different if she had lived. . . . The picture of my brother, Ludwig, in those days always hovers before me. I think sadly of what he promised at that time; how rarely charming and brilliant he was."[46]

From Frederika's account, it seems most likely that her brother turned to Judaism with such passionate observance to find solace for his profound sense of isolation that arose from his mother's death, his younger brother's death, and the compounding impact of his separation from his father in the move to live with relatives in Prague. Frederika was also deeply affected by these events, as she described:

> I told you, dear Louis, that I was twelve years old when my mother died; Ludwig was not yet eight. There followed a hard time for us children. It seemed as if all human ties were dissolving. Father could no longer get on

> with people . . . not even with his friends. He was consumed by inner anxiety. . . . He lost his patients and was irritated and depressed by the great difficulties in making a living. It was then decided to make another move. Tante Amalia, Ludwig and I went to Prague in the summer of 1842. Father was to look around. It was the first time I had seen Prague again after losing my brother there and after leaving it with my mother.[47]

Frederika wrote this in 1884. Four years earlier, she had begun this series of letters to her twenty-four-year-old son in this way:

> Dear Louis:
>
> You want me to tell you about my life and about the lives of my parents. You love to hear me talk of these things, but it is different to write of them and I'm afraid I can't do it. . . . All these things take the form of shifting pictures, really more like quickly vanishing shadows.
>
> I developed early, even though in many ways I remained a child longer than other girls. I lost my mother who was dearer to me than anything in the world and whom I idolized, when I was twelve, and I felt myself infinitely solitary and deserted. I was much alone and lived in a world which I created for myself, of my own imagination.[48]

There is a resonance in Frederika Brandeis's words with her son's observation a decade later, writing in the *Harvard Law Review,* that "the intensity and complexity of life . . . have rendered necessary some retreat from the world . . . so that solitude and privacy have become more essential to the individual."[49] I suggested earlier that this observation in Brandeis's famous article on the right to privacy could serve as a credo for his entire personal style. From his mother's letters to him, we can glimpse how this attribute was her legacy, how it derived from a deeply affecting personal loss that Brandeis himself did not directly experience, but that he nonetheless shared in an intense vicarious way.

We can see too how Lewis Dembitz, driven by the same personal imperatives that shaped his sister's inner life, offered a model for his nephew for the expression of this same attribute through Judaism generally and Zionism specifically. When Brandeis first visited Palestine in 1919 and wrote to his wife that "the ages-long longing—the love is all explicable now,"[50] there is some recapitulation of Lewis Dembitz's "joy and awe" in welcoming the Sabbath, this same "elusive something," this "Sabbath peace," this "foretaste of heaven." In Palestine, Brandeis shared the passion that his uncle Lewis had expressed in the eulogy he wrote when Theodore Herzl died in 1904: "Let us be worthy of restoration—and we will be restored to our ancient greatness."[51] In the personal losses of his mother and his uncle—grief that his mother described as a sense that "all human ties were dissolving," a feeling that she was "infinitely solitary and deserted"—we can see a basis for Louis Brandeis's passionate identification with the outcast.

This identification thus came to Brandeis as his familial heritage, as did the expression of this identification through the cultural medium of his Jewishness. It was also, however, a crucial shaping element for Brandeis that he did not directly experience the outcast status of his mother and uncle, but only shared it vicariously. This accounts for Brandeis's capacity to persist in his commitment to the outcast perspective notwithstanding its apparent adverse personal, and even general social, consequences. Brandeis's identification with outcast status was vivid but not daunting to him; he had an unshakable conviction that its difficulties could not only be borne but transcended.

I would indeed surmise that this conviction arose not only because his identification with outcast status was vicarious but also because his mother had found such satisfaction and recompense in overcoming her own childhood losses through the life she gave her children. This sense, as much as the grief of her early childhood, is clearly conveyed by Frederika's series of letters to her youngest child, Louis.[52] From this perspective, Louis might feel not only that outcast status could be transcended, but that he himself could be, perhaps even was obligated to be, an instrument of that transcendence. This too would come as his natural heritage: Brandeis's sense of mission on behalf of outsiders and his tenacious optimism that this mission could be achieved.

These two characteristics—his sense of mission and his optimism—sharply differentiated Brandeis from his colleague Holmes, the cosmically detached pessimist.[53] On this score, Frankfurter can best be understood as a hybrid of these two men. He shared Brandeis's mission, as was most visibly clear in his social reform activities (often conducted in league with Brandeis)[54] before he joined the Court. Holmes viewed this reformist zeal on the part of Brandeis and Frankfurter with amused dismissal, but neither of them was deterred.[55] When Frankfurter became a justice, however, his sense of mission faded. The conflicting elements that had previously held together in him, though in an uneasy tension, became unhinged.

Frankfurter surrendered to his passion to see himself wholeheartedly as an insider now that he had arrived at this highest imaginable social status. Precisely because he had now so wholly succumbed, any implication of failure was intolerably galling; yet he could not escape a persistent anxiety that true insider status continued to elude him.[56] Hence the bitter, unforgiving anger he directed at his brethren when they disagreed with him.[57] He could not tolerate being an outsider anywhere, least of all here in this imagined inner sanctum of American society. As he emphatically rejected any intimation that he remained an outsider, Frankfurter lost all sympathy for outsiders anywhere.

In explaining this difference between Brandeis and Frankfurter, one distinction is critically important: Frankfurter more directly experienced outcast status than Brandeis. This was true not only in the different reception of Jews in American society between Brandeis's and Frankfurter's youth and early adulthoods. It was also true in the different early social experiences of more pervasive significance for the two men: Brandeis, born in this country of a financially secure and highly educated family that gave him an easy sense of continuity between his youth and his maturity; Frankfurter, born and raised through childhood in Austria, living his adolescence on the East Side of New York City with parents of uncertain means and limited educational status, and coming to Harvard at his maturity. Frankfurter was not only more of an alien in America than Brandeis; he was also more alienated from his own family background. (This difference is suggested by one domestic detail alone: that Brandeis married his second cousin, Alice Goldmark,[58] whereas Frankfurter married the daughter of a Congregational minister "of old Yankee stock," Marion Denman.)[59]

However deeply Brandeis may have regarded himself as an outsider, however vividly he might have identified with the sufferings of his family specifically and of Jews generally, Brandeis enjoyed a luxury that was not available to Frankfurter—the luxury of vicarious, more than direct, experience of alienation. From this fundamental difference between these two men, we can draw a general lesson not only for Jews but for all Americans confronting their alienated status, their shared homelessness.

An ancient precedent in Jewish history ascribes considerable significance to the distinction between vicarious and direct experience. The distinction provides the traditional explanation of why Moses alone had the capacity to lead the Jewish people from bondage in Egypt.[60] Moses saw himself as a Jew and he empathized with their oppression; but he was not raised among them, and he was thus free from the direct influence of the spiritual degradations that they had suffered. Though Moses vicariously identified with the suffering of the Jewish slaves, he fundamentally viewed himself as a free man. He was thus able to conceive of, and to demand, freedom for his people from Pharaoh.

Moses was not, however, able to convey this conception to the Jewish people whom he led from Egypt; they were too fearful, they thought of themselves still too much as slaves. Thus, the traditional explanation posits, the Jews were condemned to wander in the desert for forty years until a new generation of Jews had come to maturity without a direct experience of slavery—with only a vicarious experience, which they in turn were expected to share with their children and their children's children by retelling the Passover story.

If Brandeis were Moses, then we might say that Frankfurter was his lieutenant Aaron—drawn from among the Jewish slaves, convinced that Moses' vision was true, but unable to sustain this conviction without Moses' personal direction in the face of popular (and his own personal) fears. Thus it was Aaron who succumbed to the populace and erected a golden idol while Moses was away on Mount Sinai receiving God's Word.[61] The basic distinction between Moses and Aaron was not in their beliefs; both men believed in the same truth. The distinction was between Moses' confidence in his own rectitude and in his people's capacity for right conduct and Aaron's lack of confidence in himself and in them.

When the Jews had finally left the desert wilderness and established themselves in Israel, this same distinction among their leaders appeared as the differentiation between the prophets and the priests. As Michael Walzer has formulated the difference:

> Whereas the priests act for the people, the prophets call upon the people to act; and whereas the priests represent the ritual requirements of the covenant, the prophets,

> denying the centrality of ritual, represent the ethical requirements. The priesthood is the vanguard grown old, the vanguard entrenched, conservative. . . . The prophets sustain the pedagogical role of Moses, though their teaching often takes the form of a savage indictment. . . . The prophets teach the law to the nation.[62]

The prophets trust the people's capacity to govern themselves in the pursuit of transcendent norms; the priests mistrust this capacity, relying on ritual and demanding popular deference to their hierarchically superior status to secure obedience to such norms. The prophets are prepared to risk social disorder because they give highest value to individual choice as the reliable route toward salvation; the priests denigrate individual choice and are prepared to impose a coerced order, albeit in supposed pursuit of the same salvational goal. If Brandeis was a prophet—Isaiah, as his contemporaries saw him—then Frankfurter was surely a high priest on the Supreme Court. In this sense, as a prophet, Brandeis sustained his identification with the outcast; and as a priest Frankfurter undertook to abandon his outcast status.

Like Moses, moreover, Brandeis had the courage to remain committed to a vision of a Promised Land while knowing that he would not attain it, that he could only pursue this homeland and not actually enter it. Brandeis, like Moses in this sense, was free from the oppressive self-satisfaction that comes with the belief that one has arrived at a safe and enviable status. From this perspective, the Jews who crossed the Jordan River into Israel, and believed they had arrived at the Promised Land, were in greater spiritual danger than Moses and his followers, who knew from their desert wandering that they remained vulnerable outcasts. The Jews who believed they had arrived were prone to smugness, to idolatrous self-worship.

In some ways the contemporary generation of American

Jews are like Moses and Brandeis. This generation for the most part was born in America and has not been scarred by the pervasive anti-Semitism that their parents confronted. In this sense, for the contemporary generation of American Jews, bondage is a vicarious, rather than direct, experience. The vicarious experience is extraordinarily vivid, as the memory of the Holocaust and the current threats to the existence of the state of Israel testify. But, like Brandeis and like Moses, American Jews are more favorably situated than others; they bear witness from a more secure vantage point.

If American Jews do see themselves as outcasts notwithstanding their apparent security, then their Jewishness offers a medium for the expression of this identification. This was Brandeis's way: that he saw himself first as homeless and then as a Jew and a Zionist. But, as for Brandeis, the question of whether American Jews today should identify themselves with outcasts cannot be answered by self-evident reference to their status as Jews. For this generation, identification with the suffering of outcasts requires an act of will, a bold imagining, more than an inevitable, forced acknowledgment.

In their apparent security, contemporary American Jews have more in common with most other Americans today than with outcasts in this country or elsewhere. In this sense, like Frankfurter, contemporary American Jews may believe they have found their Promised Land, and they are accordingly vulnerable to the temptations of idolatrous self-worship. Indeed, most Americans are as prone to this false comfort, to turning away from any identification with outcasts, as are most American Jews.[63] The lesson taught by Moses and by Brandeis, however, is that no one is truly capable of denying kinship with outcasts.

Many people believe they are able to deny this kinship. Their denial has all the trappings of an assured reality, as reflected in the apparent solidity of pharaonic courts and armies.

But in the end this is an assurance built on sand. This end inevitably comes in the effort to sustain a clear distance between outsider and insider.

The effort can appear successful for long periods, sometimes even for generations. It is nonetheless afflicted by everyone's tacit understanding that progressively increased resistance and then open brutality directed against outsiders is required to maintain the solidity of the boundary lines; and this effort necessarily leads to increasing insecurity and then open terror among the putative insiders.[64]

The existence of this dynamic can sometimes be ignored. But if the social experience of the putative insiders has led them to suspect, for whatever reasons, that the distance between them and the outcasts is challengeable, then an escalating dynamic of repression and fear intrudes with increasing insistence. Brandeis and Frankfurter shared this starting point—that their social experiences, however varied, taught them both that the distinction between denizen of a safe haven and despised outcast is not invariably and assuredly settled. Their gentile contemporaries may not have learned this lesson with equal vividness; but no one in America today can avoid acknowledging this lesson, this starting place for charting a social and personal course.

From this initial point, Brandeis and Frankfurter drew diametrically opposed lessons. Brandeis acknowledged a basic identity with outcasts and consistently tried to dissolve the distinction between inside and outside; Frankfurter insisted on maintaining the distinction and devoted progressively increased personal and social force to the enterprise. This same contrast is apparent in comparing the actions of the Supreme Court majority today with its immediate predecessor. The paradigmatic expression of the Warren Court majority was its attempt to dissolve outcast status implicit in *Brown v. Board of Education.* For our time the paradigm is the series of cases from *Furman* in 1972, which acknowledged doubts about the rationality of the death penalty, to the Court's current decisions not resolving these doubts but endeavoring to suppress their acknowledgment by closing off both procedural opportunities and substantive grounds for federal and state court review.[65]

This forced suppression of doubts about the fairness or rationality of the fixed boundary between insider and outcast status, as currently represented by the death penalty, preoccupied Frankfurter during his tenure as a Supreme Court justice. It is the chosen path of the Court majority today and, it seems, of a majority of Americans not only regarding the death penalty but in other boundary issues concerning race and economic class relations. This path promises no reliable social peace. Nor does it offer personal repose.

A lesson emerges from the contrasting careers of these two Jewish justices. Frankfurter struggled against acknowledging his outcast status, but vainly; and he always remained homeless in spite of himself. Brandeis embraced homelessness as his heritage, and he drew strength from it. Brandeis's example is more difficult to follow day by day, but it is ultimately more rewarding.

Notes

1. Diaspora Jew

1. The other lectures delivered on that occasion—one by Monroe Price, also a friend and law school classmate, now dean at Cardozo Law School, the other by a newer friend, Saul Touster of Brandeis University—were published in 33 BUFFALO L. REV. 562, 571 (1984).

2. In writing this book I have relied almost exclusively on published sources regarding both Brandeis and Frankfurter. So many of the private papers of both men have been published and the unpublished materials have been so thoroughly combed and described by so many different scholars that I felt justified in thus restricting my research. I did make a few forays into unpublished archival materials and found useful material in Frankfurter's unpublished notes of conversations with Brandeis. Soon after I obtained a copy of these notes from the Harvard Law School Brandeis collection, however, even they appeared in print (see M. Urofsky, "The Brandeis-Frankfurter Conversations," 1985 SUP. CT. REV. 299); and my initial conclusion that the published sources on these two men were extensive enough for my purposes was reinforced.

3. See J. Morris, "The American Jewish Judge: An Appraisal on the Occasion of the Bicentennial," 38 JEWISH SOCIAL STUDIES 195 (1976).

4. See generally A. GOODHART, FIVE JEWISH LAWYERS OF THE COMMON LAW (London: Jewish Historical Society of England, 1949) 4–15; C. MADISON, EMINENT AMERICAN JEWS: 1776 TO THE PRESENT (New York: Frederick Unger, 1970) 42–56.

2. Brandeis

1. A. T. Mason, Brandeis: A Free Man's Life (New York: Viking, 1946) 66–67.

2. B. Weinryb, "Jewish Immigration and Accommodation to America," in The Jews: Social Patterns of an American Group (M. Sklare, ed.) (New York: Free Press, 1958) 627.

3. *Id.* at 13.

4. See Mason, *supra* note 1, at 11–22. See also J. Goldmark, Pilgrims of '48 (New Haven: Yale Univ. Press, 1930) 169.

5. P. Strum, Louis D. Brandeis: Justice for the People (Cambridge, Mass.: Harvard Univ. Press, 1984) 36–37, 228–29.

6. Brandeis himself wrote at the time, in the third person, "The dominant reasons for the opposition to the confirmation of Mr. Brandeis are that he is considered a radical and is a Jew." See Strum, *id.*, at 293–94.

7. See Weinryb, *supra* note 2, at 15–16; I. Howe, World of Our Fathers (New York: Harcourt Brace Jovanovich, 1976) 58–63.

8. Mason, *supra* note 1, at 444.

9. *Id.* at 445. The full text appears in J. de Haas, Louis D. Brandeis: A Biographical Sketch (New York: Bloch, 1929) 161–62.

10. See generally M. Urofsky, American Zionism from Herzl to the Holocaust (Garden City, N.Y.: Doubleday, Anchor Books, 1975) 144–50.

11. Strum, *supra* note 5, at 248–49, 254–55.

12. Mason, *supra* note 1, at 512.

13. Urofsky, *supra* note 10, at 273.

14. Mason, *supra* note 1, at 464.

15. Statement of Austen G. Fox, quoted in *id.* at 506.

16. See *id.* at 105–6.

17. *Id.* at 103.

18. D. Levy, "The Lawyer as Judge: Brandeis' View of the Legal Profession," 22 Okla. L. Rev. 374, 390–91 (1969).

19. 277 U.S. 438, 478 (1928).

20. C. Warren and L. Brandeis, "The Right to Privacy," 4 Harvard L. Rev. 193 (1890).

21. *Id.* at 220.

22. *Id.* at 196.

23. See STRUM, *supra* note 5, at 339–53.

24. D. ACHESON, MORNING AND NOON (Boston: Houghton Mifflin, 1965) 51.

25. STRUM, *supra* note 5, at 357.

26. MASON, *supra* note 1, at 79.

27. The full content of this observation is worth quotation. Holmes was asking Laski

> whether loveableness is a characteristic of the better class of Jews. When I think how many of the younger men that have warmed my heart have been Jews I cannot but suspect, and I put the question to you. Brandeis, whom many dislike, seems to me to have this quality and always gives me a glow, even though I am not sure. . . . [Holmes then envisions the prospect of his burning at the "low fire" referred to in the text, and continues:] I don't for a moment doubt that for daily purposes he feels to me as a friend—as certainly I do to him and without the above reserve. This, of course, *strictissime* between ourselves. I pause to remark that I have a scarf pin that gives me immense pleasure—it looks so like a cockroach hiding in a corner with a gleam of light upon his back. While interrogating you let me ask whether you think as it sometimes is said that the Jews always have No. 1 at the bottom more than the rest of the world. I put these things to you as one capable of detached opinions.
>
> Letter of 12 January 1921, HOLMES-LASKI LETTERS (M. Howe, ed.) (Cambridge, Mass.: Harvard Univ. Press, 1953) 304–5

There is no record of Laski's direct response to Holmes's question.

28. MASON, *supra* note 1, at 80.

29. Duplex Printing Press Co. v. Deering, 254 U.S. 443, 488 (1921).

30. UROFSKY, *supra* note 10, at 291–94.

31. Quoted in L. BAKER, BRANDEIS AND FRANKFURTER: A DUAL BIOGRAPHY (New York: Harper & Row, 1984) 179.

32. UROFSKY, *supra* note 10, at 267, 280.

33. See C. WEIZMANN, TRIAL AND ERROR (New York: Harper &

Row, 1949) 267 ("The propositions of the Brandeis group . . . reflected a denial of Jewish nationalism; they made of Zionism simply a sociological plan . . . instead of the folk renaissance that it was").

34. UROFSKY, *supra* note 10, at 294.

35. *Id.* at 297.

36. Brandeis remained personally committed to Zionism even after he had resigned from the Zionist movement. He was eagerly welcomed back and rejoined the American Zionist Organization in 1930, though again defeating the expectation of some that he would at last resign from the Court and assume their leadership. *Id.* at 367–69.

37. Quoted in *id.* at 33.

38. See B. HALPERN, THE AMERICAN JEW: A ZIONIST ANALYSIS (New York: Schocken Books, 1983) 26, 126–27.

39. UROFSKY, *supra* note 10, at 131.

40. See M. UROFSKY, A MIND OF ONE PIECE: BRANDEIS AND AMERICAN REFORM (New York: Charles Scribner's Sons, 1971) 100–101.

41. DE HAAS, *supra* note 9, at 163.

42. MASON, *supra* note 1, at 457.

43. MASON, *supra* note 1, at 458.

44. Letter of 5 October 1919, HOLMES-LASKI LETTERS, *supra* note 27, at 212.

45. Compare Harold Laski's judgment, conveyed in a letter to Holmes: "[Brandeis] is really a Jeffersonian Democrat, trying to use the power of the State to enforce an environment in which competition may be really free and equal; this I take to be an impossible task. Secondly, his method of analysis does magnificently relate law to the life of which it is the expression; third, his criterion for all action is an ethical individualism. I take him to be intellectually, as to ends, a romantic anachronism, but as to methods a really significant figure in the Court. . . . I conclude that his contribution has been that of a good and big man. A prophet, I suspect, rather than a judge; a grand player for a side in which he believes both disinterestedly and with all his might." Letter of 12 August 1933, *id.* at 1448. See also A. BICKEL, THE UNPUBLISHED OPINIONS OF MR. JUSTICE BRANDEIS (Chicago: Univ. of Chicago Press, 1957) 121–24; T. MCCRAW, PROPHETS OF REGULATION (Cambridge, Mass.: Harvard Univ. Press, 1984) 108–9, 138–41.

46. See S. KONEFSKY, THE LEGACY OF HOLMES AND BRANDEIS (New York: Macmillan, 1956) 140, 162–69.

47. See Y. Rogat, "The Judge as Spectator," 31 U. CHI. L. REV. 213 (1964).

48. W. Mendelson, "The Influence of James B. Thayer upon the Work of Holmes, Brandeis and Frankfurter," 31 VAND. L. REV. 71, 75 (1978).

49. ACHESON, *supra* note 24, at 95–96.

50. For Holmes's view, see, e.g., Lochner v. New York, 198 U.S. 45, 76 (1905) (dissenting opinion), Hammer v. Dagenhart, 247 U.S. 251, 280–81 (1918) (dissenting opinion), O. W. HOLMES, COLLECTED LEGAL PAPERS (New York: P. Smith, 1953) 258 ("Wise or not, the proximate test of a good government is that the dominant power has its way").

51. See Mendelson, *supra* note 48.

52. Letter of 13 December 1930, quoted in BICKEL, *supra* note 45, at 222. In an earlier exchange, Laski had written that Roscoe Pound of the Harvard Law School "spoke rather strongly as to the advocate in B[randeis] being over-prominent in his decisions just as in his general philosophy." Letter of 13 January 1918, HOLMES-LASKI LETTERS, *supra* note 27, at 127. Holmes had responded, "On one occasion I told [Brandeis] that I thought he was letting partisanship disturb his judicial attitude." Letter of 18 January 1918, *id.* at 128.

53. Frankfurter, "Mr. Justice Brandeis and the Constitution," in MR. JUSTICE BRANDEIS (F. Frankfurter, ed.) (New Haven: Yale Univ. Press, 1932) 117.

54. See H. Wechsler, "Toward Neutral Principles of Constitutional Law," 73 HARV. L. REV. 1 (1959).

55. Quoted in STRUM, *supra* note 5, at 346.

56. 254 U.S. 504 (1924).

57. 254 U.S. at 517.

58. 254 U.S. at 533–34.

59. See G. Gunther, "In Search of Evolving Doctrine on a Changing Court: A Model for a Newer Equal Protection," 86 HARV. L. REV. 1, 21 (1972).

60. Quoted in STRUM, *supra* note 5, at 108–9.

61. Quoted in A. GAL, BRANDEIS OF BOSTON (Cambridge, Mass.: Harvard Univ. Press, 1980) 126.

62. Compare Dean Acheson's observation: "Justice Brandeis was not a simple man. His approach to his opinions was not a simple one, was not aimed merely to produce a scholarly and sound rationalization of the Court's decision. Opinions were addressed to two audiences—first, to his colleagues on the Court, and, second, to counsel in the cases and the bar beyond them. In dissent he often had another audience also in mind, the politically sophisticated public. . . . The purpose was education and persuasion; the method, that of education—patience, repetition, understanding the interests of the learner and meeting them." ACHESON, *supra* note 24, at 83.

63. See KONEFSKY, *supra* note 46, at 76.

64. Panama Refining Co. v. Ryan, 293 U.S. 430 (1935), Humphrey's Executor v. United States, 295 U.S. 602 (1935), Louisville Bank v. Radford, 295 U.S. 555 (1935), Schechter Poultry Co. v. United States, 295 U.S. 528 (1935).

65. Harry Hopkins, "Statement to Me by Thomas Corcoran Giving His Recollection of the Genesis of the Supreme Court Fight," 3 April 1939, quoted in A. SCHLESINGER, JR., THE POLITICS OF UPHEAVAL (Boston: Houghton Mifflin, 1960) 280.

66. Though Frankfurter had not yet joined the Court, he apparently disagreed with Brandeis's position in these cases; the precise reason for this disagreement was not, however, clear. Both Frankfurter and Brandeis had been opposed to the enactment of the NRA, but in 1935 Frankfurter appeared to take the position that the Court should not have constitutionally invalidated it; Brandeis's vote was the occasion for unusual strain in their relationship. See N. DAWSON, LOUIS D. BRANDEIS, FELIX FRANKFURTER AND THE NEW DEAL (Hamden, Conn.: Archon Books, 1980) 128–34. Nonetheless, it is possible that Frankfurter's criticism of Brandeis did not in this instance so much rest on differing conceptions of the judicial role as on Frankfurter's ambition to attain a judicial role by safeguarding his close relationship with Franklin Roosevelt.

67. See Y. Rogat, "Mr. Justice Holmes: A Dissenting Opinion," 15 STAN. L. REV. 3, 9 (1962).

68. As Holmes wrote to Brandeis in 1919: "Generally speaking, I agree with you in liking to see social experiments tried but I do so without enthusiasm because I believe it is merely shifting the pressure and that so long as we have free propagation Malthus is right in his general view." Quoted in BICKEL, *supra* note 45, at 221.

69. See Konefsky, *supra* note 46, at 140.

70. 262 U.S. 390 (1923).

71. *Id.* at 401.

72. *Id.* at 412.

73. Compare Brandeis's dissenting observation in New State Ice Co. v. Liebman, 285 U.S. 262, 311 (1932): "Denial of the right to experiment may be fraught with serious consequences to the Nation. It is one of the happy incidents of the federal system that a single courageous State may, if its citizens choose, serve as a laboratory; and try novel social and economic experiments without risk to the rest of the country. This Court has the power to prevent an experiment [Brandeis appended a footnote here: Compare Felix Frankfurter, "The Public and Its Government," pp. 49–51]. . . . But in the exercise of this high power, we must ever be on our guard, lest we erect our prejudices into legal principles."

74. Urofsky, "The Brandeis-Frankfurter Conversations," 1985 Sup. Ct. Rev. 299, 320.

75. Mason, *supra* note 1, at 26, 647 n. 11.

76. Frankfurter also disagreed with Brandeis and endorsed Holmes's dissent in *Meyer,* in a *New Republic* editorial. See Felix Frankfurter on the Supreme Court (P. Kurland, ed.) (Cambridge, Mass.: Harvard Univ. Press, 1970) 174–78.

77. Two years later the Court applied the *Meyer* precedent to strike down a state law forbidding private elementary education; this time Holmes silently concurred—most likely not because he had altered his dissenting views from *Meyer* but because he was usually unwilling to repeat his dissents once his view had been clearly rejected by a Court majority. See M. Kelman, "The Forked Path of Dissent," 1985 Sup. Ct. Rev. 227, 256.

78. 254 U.S. at 534.

79. See Acheson, *supra* note 24, at 94.

80. See Bickel, *supra* note 45, at 77–99.

81. *Id.* at 85.

82. *Id.* at 85–86.

83. *Id.* at 86–88.

84. *Id.* at 97.

85. *Ibid.*

86. Mason, *supra* note 1, at 470, 489–90.

87. *Id.* at 537–39.

88. *Id.* at 514.

89. STRUM, *supra* note 5, at 294.

90. See GAL, *supra* note 61; Yonathan Shapiro, "American Jews in Politics: The Case of Louis D. Brandeis," 15 AMER. JEWISH HIST. QUART. 199 (1965).

91. UROFSKY, *supra* note 40, at 101–3; STRUM, *supra* note 5, at 225–34.

92. Allon Gal concludes that Brandeis "made [a] somewhat thwarted attempt to join the clubs and generally live the life of the Brahmins" by residing in the Yankee stronghold of Dedham and, through Warren's sponsorship, joining the Dedham Polo Club to "mix . . . with the most elite of Boston society." GAL, *supra* note 61, at 122–23. Gal, *id.* at 39, cites a letter written in 1916, after Brandeis's nomination to the Court, by a "well-connected and well-informed Brahmin":

> I knew him some twenty-five years ago, when the influence of Sam Warren got him into the Dedham Polo Club. It was a club of gentlemen, and Brandeis was soon conspicuously left to "flock by himself," with the result that he ceased to frequent the club and his absence was not regretted.

Gal continues:

> Brandeis, left to "flock by himself" at the Polo Club, took up solitary pursuits such as walking and canoeing and apparently also sought the company of children in a way that his natural disposition would not have suggested. People who cannot recall their parents' ever dining with his family do remember Brandeis speaking to them as children about their play, what they were reading, and their opinions on various topics.

While anti-Semitism was undoubtedly increasingly marked in Dedham, as in all of American society, during the years of Brandeis's residence there, I believe Gal misconstrues Brandeis's personal disposition in concluding that "thwarted" social ambition drove him reluctantly to "solitary pursuits." Gal also implies that Brandeis's decision to live apart from the Jewish families of Boston, though he cultivated them as clients, reflected his ambition of Yankee acceptance. But this too can be understood—and I believe more plausibly—as a reflection of Brandeis's own personal inclinations. Gal states, "The Brandeises' social isolation in Dedham . . . tell[s] us a good deal about the life of a Jewish family in a Yankee town." *Id.* at 39. Perhaps so; but in Brandeis's case, I think it tells us more about him than about his Yankee neighbors' attitudes toward him.

3. Frankfurter

1. J. Lash, From the Diaries of Felix Frankfurter (New York: Norton, 1975) (hereafter Diaries) 30.

2. Letter of 24 September 1925, quoted in B. Murphy, The Brandeis/Frankfurter Connection (Garden City, N.Y.: Doubleday, Anchor Books, 1983) 39.

3. I. Berlin, Personal Impressions (New York: Viking, 1981) 84, 87.

4. Mason, *supra,* chap. 2, note 26.

5. Diaries, *supra* note 1, at 30. See also Dean Acheson's account of his daily walks to work with Frankfurter: "As time went on, our inability to stop our talk at the Pennsylvania Avenue entrance to the old State Department Building led to amused comment, which drove us to an agreement that we would stop, even in the middle of a sentence, as we passed a certain crack in the sidewalk. But it was no use. He claimed that to stop walking, but not talking, was only proper avoidance, and not illegal evasion, of the rule." D. Acheson, Fragments of My Fleece (New York: Norton, 1971) 221.

6. J. Rauh, "Felix Frankfurter: Civil Libertarian," Harv. Civ. Rts.–Civ. Lib. L. Rev. 496, 513 (1976).

7. Diaries, *supra* note 1, at 89; see also *id.* at 63. Compare Acheson's observation, *supra* note 5, at 220: "One needs to see, to hear—particularly to hear his laugh, his general noisiness—to realize what an obstreperous person this man is, to have one's arm numbed by his vise-like grip just above one's elbow, to feel the intensity of his nervous energy."

8. Berlin, *supra* note 3, at 85.

9. Felix Frankfurter Reminisces (H. Phillips, ed.) (New York: Reynal, 1960) (hereafter Reminisces) 289–90.

10. Murphy, *supra* note 2, at 287–88.

11. Baker, *supra,* chap. 2, note 31, at 41–42.

12. Reminisces, *supra* note 9, at 4–5.

13. See Howe, *supra,* chap. 2, note 7, at 261–78.

14. Diaries, *supra* note 1, at 20.

15. Roosevelt and Frankfurter: Their Correspondence, 1928–1945 (M. Freedman, ed.) (Boston: Little, Brown, 1967) 744.

16. Diaries, *supra* note 1, at 264.

17. Reminisces, *supra* note 9, at 19.

18. Diaries, *supra* note 1, at 211–12.

19. 320 U.S. 118 (1943).

20. 310 U.S. 586 (1940).

21. P. Freund, "Charles Evans Hughes as Chief Justice," 81 Harv. L. Rev. 4, 41 (1967).

22. R. Danzig, "Justice Frankfurter's Opinions in the Flag Salute Cases: Blending Logic and Psychologic in Constitutional Decisionmaking," 36 Stan. L. Rev. 675, 710 (1984).

23. 310 U.S. at 599, 597. Holmes advanced this same jurisprudential rationale, which Frankfurter endorsed at the time, in Meyer v. Nebraska, 262 U.S. 390 (1923), regarding the state law prohibiting German language elementary school education; see *supra,* chap. 2, note 76. Frankfurter's judgment that the statute in *Meyer* was "reasonable" may have been colored by his favorable recollections of Miss Hogan's impositions on him (just as Brandeis's disapproval of the statute was perhaps affected by his use of German in his early education).

24. 310 U.S. at 599–600.

25. *Id.* at 598.

26. *Ibid.*

27. *Id.* at 591, 596.

28. *Supra,* chap. 2, notes 50, 54.

29. West Virginia State Board of Education v. Barnette, 319 U.S. 624, 646–47 (1943).

30. Diaries, *supra* note 1, at 254.

31. Danzig, *supra* note 22, at 702–3.

32. See *infra,* chap. 5, notes 23–31 and accompanying text.

33. Reminisces, *supra* note 9, at 276.

34. *Ibid.*

35. Adamson v. California, 332 U.S. 46, 67 (1947) (concurring opinion).

36. 330 U.S. 258 (1947).

37. 330 U.S. at 308–9.

38. Diaries, *supra* note 1, at 67.

39. *Id.* at 68.

40. *Id.* at 70–71; Rauh, *supra* note 6, at 505.

41. Diaries, *supra* note 1, at xi.

42. 319 U.S. at 664–65.

43. 319 U.S. at 642–43.

44. 358 U.S. 1 (1958).

45. E. Warren, Memoirs 298 (Garden City, N.Y.: Doubleday, 1977).

46. *Id.* at 298–99.

47. D. Hutchinson, "Unanimity and Desegregation: Decision-making in the Supreme Court, 1948–1958," 68 Geo. L. J. 1, 83 n.705 (1979).

48. *Id.* at 83 n.707.

49. *Id.* at 83.

50. *Ibid.*

51. *Id.* at 84.

52. 358 U.S. at 20.

53. 347 U.S. 483 (1954).

54. D. Hutchinson, "Felix Frankfurter and the Business of the Supreme Court, O.T. 1946–O.T. 1961," 1980 Sup. Ct. Rev. 143, at 169, 184.

55. See B. Schwartz, "Felix Frankfurter and Earl Warren: A Study of a Deteriorating Relationship," 1980 Sup. Ct. Rev. 115.

56. Reminisces, *supra* note 9, at 233.

57. *Id.* at 253.

58. *Id.* at 254.

59. *Id.* at 254–55.

60. *Id.* at 255.

61. D. Bryden, "Brandeis's Facts," 1 Constitutional Commentary 281, 304–5 (1984).

62. Diaries, *supra* note 1, at 25–26.

63. *Id.* at 24–25.

64. See Frankfurter's letter in 1937 noting that he was "the symbol of the Jew, the 'red', the 'alien.'" Quoted in Baker, *supra,* chap. 2, note 31, at 326.

65. Reminisces, *supra* note 9, at 202–3.
66. *Id.* at 213.
67. Baker, *supra,* chap. 2, note 31, at 231.
68. 250 U.S. 616 (1919).
69. Reminisces, *supra* note 9, at 177.
70. Diaries, *supra* note 1, at 66.

4. Pariah or Parvenu

1. H. Arendt, The Origins of Totalitarianism (1951; reprint, New York: Harcourt Brace Jovanovich, 1973) 56–68.

2. Compare Eleanor Roosevelt's initial reaction to Frankfurter in a letter to her mother-in-law after she had met him in 1918: "An interesting little man but very jew." Quoted in Diaries, *supra,* chap. 3, note 1, at 24.

3. *Supra,* chap. 2, notes 15, 49.

4. Arendt, *supra* note 1, at 68–79.

5. *Id.* at 75.

6. Compare the letter sent to Brandeis in 1901 by his first law partner, Samuel Warren: "You have encouraged our right impulses and criticized our faults with an unbiased discernment which could only come from outside. In many ways you are a better example of New England virtue than the natives." Quoted in Mason, *supra,* chap. 2, note 1, at 389. See also Gal, *supra,* chap. 2, note 61, at 84–85, citing "the philo-Semitic attitude . . . alive in Boston" around 1900 and quoting Brandeis's "good friend Elizabeth Evans . . . [on] learning that Brandeis was a Jew [responding] that 'it gave an aroma to his personality. A Jew! He belonged then to Isaiah and the Prophets.'"

7. Arendt, *supra* note 1, at 69.

8. Urofsky, *supra,* chap. 2, note 37.

9. Arendt, *supra* note 1, at 70.

10. Mason *supra,* chap. 2, note 9.

11. Arendt, *supra* note 1, at 71.

12. A. De Tocqueville, Democracy in America (1835–39; reprint, Garden City, N.Y.: Doubleday, 1969) 268. In the first Congress, convened in 1789, 38 percent of both the Senate and House were lawyers, whereas planters or landholders totaled 48 percent of

the Senate and 36 percent of the House. Lawyers were the single largest occupational group in the 100th Congress, convened in 1987: 62 percent of the Senate and 42 percent of the House. *New York Times,* 5 January 1987, at A14, col. 1.

13. See J. Auerbach, "From Rags to Robes: The Legal Profession, Social Mobility and the American Jewish Experience," 26 AMER. JEWISH HIST. QUART. 253, 273–74 (1976).

14. S. Lipset and E. Ladd, "Jewish Academics in the United States: Their Achievements, Culture and Politics," 72 AMERICAN JEWISH YEARBOOK, 89, 95 (1971); C. SILBERMAN, A CERTAIN PEOPLE 100 (New York: Summit Books, 1985). At this same time, Jews comprised about 10 percent of the legal profession generally, according to an estimate provided by the American Section of the International Association of Jewish Lawyers and Jurists.

15. STRUM, *supra,* chap. 2, note 5, at 359–60.

16. SILBERMAN, *supra* note 14, at 99–100.

17. Letter of 13 October 1929, in LETTERS OF LOUIS D. BRANDEIS 5:404 (M. I. Urofsky and D. W. Levy, eds.) (Albany, N.Y.: SUNY Press, 1978).

18. I. BERLIN, JEWISH SLAVERY AND EMANCIPATION (New York: Herzl Press, 1961) 7–12, 15.

19. SILBERMAN, *supra* note 14, at 119–24.

20. For differing views on this issue, compare SILBERMAN, *id.* at 82–116, with HALPERN, *supra,* chap. 2, note 38, at 175–78.

21. Richard Hofstadter sees this nostalgic wish for recapturing vanished virtues and social conditions taking dominant hold in late-nineteenth-century America:

> Beginning with the time of [William Jennings] Bryan, the dominant American ideal has been steadily fixed on bygone institutions and conditions. In early twentieth-century progressivism this backward-looking vision reached the dimensions of a major paradox. Such heroes of the progressive revival as Bryan, La Follette, and Wilson proclaimed that they were trying to undo the mischief of the past forty years and re-create the old nation of limited and decentralized power, genuine competition, democratic opportunity, and enterprise. As Wilson put it, the machinery of democratic government was to be revivified "*for the purpose of recovering what seems to have been*

> *lost* . . . our *old* variety and freedom and individual energy of development."
>
> R. Hofstadter, The American Political Tradition (New York: Random House, Vintage Books, 1960) vi–vii

David Rothman, tracing the origins of asylums for various stripes of deviants in Jacksonian America, sees the same kind of nostalgic wish to recapture an imagined past era—to "re-create fixity and stability" such as eighteenth-century America had supposedly achieved. D. Rothman, The Discovery of the Asylum (Boston: Little, Brown, 1971) 133. See also P. Boyer, Urban Masses and Moral Order in America, 1820–1930 (Cambridge, Mass.: Harvard Univ. Press, 1978) 3–4. In his study of prerevolutionary Virginia, Rhys Isaac identifies a similar romanticized longing in the 1760s for the imagined virtues of the early eighteenth century in America. R. Isaac, The Transformation of Virginia, 1740–1790, (Chapel Hill: Univ. of North Carolina Press, 1982) 143–205.

As Samuel P. Huntington summarizes the matter,

> During both the Revolutionary and Jacksonian years, the articulation of American political ideals was couched to some degree in conservative and backward-looking terms, as a reaffirmation of rights which had previously existed and as an effort to reorder political life in terms of principles whose legitimacy had been previously established. During the Progressive era, the backward-looking characteristics of the ideals and vision that were invoked stood out much more sharply.
>
> S. Huntington, American Politics: The Promise of Disharmony (Cambridge, Mass.: Harvard Univ. Press, 1981) 226

22. Compare Freud's observation:

> Originally the ego includes everything, later it separates off an external world from itself. Our present ego-feeling is, therefore, only a shrunken residue of a much more inclusive—indeed, an all-embracing—feeling which corresponded to a more intimate bond between the ego and the world about it. If we may assume that there are many people in whose mental life this primary ego-feeling has persisted to a greater or less de-

> gree, it would exist in them side by side with the narrower and more sharply demarcated ego-feeling of maturity, like a kind of counterpart to it. . . . But have we a right to assume the survival of something that was originally there, alongside of what was later derived from it? Undoubtedly. There is nothing strange in such a phenomenon, whether in the mental field or elsewhere.
>
> S. FREUD, CIVILIZATION AND ITS DISCONTENTS (1930; reprint, New York: Norton, 1962) 15

23. See R. BELLAH et al., HABITS OF THE HEART: INDIVIDUALISM AND COMMITMENT IN AMERICAN LIFE (Berkeley and Los Angeles: Univ. of California Press, 1985) 55–163.

24. One-quarter of all marriages in 1960 resulted in divorce; by 1970 this proportion had increased to one-third and by 1980 to one-half. U.S. BUREAU OF THE CENSUS, STATISTICAL ABSTRACT OF THE UNITED STATES: 1986 (106th ed.), table 124. Moreover, "the total number of children affected by divorce has more than tripled since 1960. . . . It is now projected that *more than half of all children in the United States* will experience a parental divorce or dissolution before they reach age eighteen." L. WEITZMAN, THE DIVORCE REVOLUTION: THE UNEXPECTED SOCIAL AND ECONOMIC CONSEQUENCES FOR WOMEN AND CHILDREN IN AMERICA (New York: Free Press, 1985) (emphasis in original) 215.

25. About six million people, or 3 percent of the population, moved between states each year between 1960 and 1980; the same number moved each of these years between counties in the same state. STATISTICAL ABSTRACT, *supra* note 24, table 15.

26. See G. MYRDAL, AN AMERICAN DILEMMA (New York: Harper & Row, 1944) 191–201, 879–82.

27. King ended his speech on 28 August 1963 with hope for "that day when all of God's children—black men and white men, Jews and Gentiles, Protestants and Catholics—will be able to join hands and sing in the words of the old Negro spiritual, 'Free at last. Free at last. Thank God Almighty, we are free at last.'"

28. B. FRIEDAN, THE FEMININE MYSTIQUE (New York: Norton, 1974) 379–85; National Organization for Women, "Statement of Purpose," in SISTERHOOD IS POWERFUL (R. Morgan, ed.) (New York:

Random House, 1970) 512–14. See ACCESS TO POWER: CROSS-NATIONAL STUDIES OF WOMEN AND ELITES (C. Epstein and R. Coser, eds.) (Boston: Allen & Unwin, 1981).

29. See M. WOLLSTONECRAFT, A VINDICATION OF THE RIGHTS OF WOMEN (London: J. Johnson, 1792). See also E. C. Stanton, "Home Life," reprinted in ELIZABETH CADY STANTON AND SUSAN B. ANTHONY: SELECTED DOCUMENTS (E. DuBois, ed.) (New York: Schocken Books, 1981) 131–38; A. Rossi, "Woman of Action: Frances Wright," in THE FEMINIST PAPERS FROM ADAMS TO DE BEAUVOIR (A. Rossi, ed.) (New York: Columbia Univ. Press, 1973) 93.

30. See S. ROTHMAN, A WOMAN'S PROPER PLACE: A HISTORY OF CHANGING IDEALS AND PRACTICE, 1870 TO THE PRESENT (New York: Basic Books, 1978) 179–80; C. LASCH, HAVEN IN A HEARTLESS WORLD: THE FAMILY BESIEGED (New York: Basic Books, 1977) 5–9, 37–43; K. SKLAR, CATHARINE BEECHER: A STUDY IN AMERICAN DOMESTICITY (New Haven: Yale Univ. Press, 1973) 161–63.

31. See C. GILLIGAN, IN A DIFFERENT VOICE: PSYCHOLOGICAL THEORY AND WOMEN'S DEVELOPMENT (Cambridge, Mass.: Harvard Univ. Press, 1982); E. Janeway, "Women and the Uses of Power," in THE FUTURE OF DIFFERENCE (H. Eisenstein and A. Jardine, eds.) (Boston: G. K. Hall, 1980) 327–45.

32. Richard Hofstadter has seen this kind of protest as a recurrent phenomenon in our culture. See R. HOFSTADTER, THE PARANOID STYLE IN AMERICAN POLITICS (New York: Random House, Vintage Books, 1967) 3–40.

33. See A. SCULL, DECARCERATION: COMMUNITY TREATMENT AND THE DEVIANT, A RADICAL VIEW (Englewood Cliffs, N.J.: Prentice-Hall, 1977) 95–98; T. SZASZ, THE AGE OF MADNESS (Garden City, N.Y.: Doubleday, Anchor Books, 1973) xi–xiii.

34. See T. SZASZ, THE MYTH OF MENTAL ILLNESS (New York: Hueber-Harper, 1961) 40–45, 145–47; A. MASTERS, BEDLAM (London: Michael Joseph, 1977) 14–16; R. PERRUCCI, CIRCLE OF MADNESS: ON BEING INSANE AND INSTITUTIONALIZED IN AMERICA (Englewood Cliffs, N.J.: Prentice-Hall, 1974) 14–18.

35. "For Mentally Ill, Life on Streets Is No Boon," *New York Times,* 4 January 1987, at E7, col. 3.

36. ARENDT, *supra* note 1, 347–54, 437–44.

37. O. PATTERSON, SLAVERY AND SOCIAL DEATH (Cambridge, Mass.: Harvard Univ. Press, 1982) 5–13.

38. The germ of this idea can be discerned in Karl Marx's conclusion in his infamous essay "On the Jewish Question" that all Christian society had been "reabsorbed into Judaism" because society had "dissolve[d] . . . into a world of atomistic, antagonistic individuals." THE MARX-ENGELS READER (R. Tucker, ed.) (New York: Norton, 1972) 50. Marx viewed both Christian society generally and Jews specifically with such hatred that the analytic usefulness of this proposition was obscured by the virulence of his descriptive formulation of it. Thus Marx maintained that the "profane basis of Judaism" was "self-interest," that the "worldly cult of the Jew" was accordingly "huckstering" and "his worldly god" was "money." *Id.* at 46. All these attributes, Marx further maintained, had become broadly characteristic of capitalist bourgeois society generally.

Stripping away the viciously caricatured anti-Semitism in Marx's formulation, the plausible underlying sense of his observation could be stated thus: The relations between European Jews and Christians had not been based on pervasive social bonding but only on a narrow and transitory nexus of commercial self-interest; as social relations within Christian Europe changed (from "feudal" to "capitalist" social structures, as he would put it), the commercial nexus—"a world [populated by] atomistic, antagonistic individuals"—became the dominant basis for all relationships; hence, social relations within all European society came to resemble the previous relations between European Christians and Jews. In this sense, then, Marx was observing that all Europe had become populated by alienated outcasts, the status once reserved for Jews. Marx distorted this observation, however, through the lens of his ferocious hatreds. See Isaiah Berlin's essay, "Benjamin Disraeli, Karl Marx and the Search for Identity," in I. BERLIN, AGAINST THE CURRENT (New York: Viking, 1980) 277, 282–84.

39. See HALPERN, *supra,* chap. 2, note 38, at 26–33.

40. See generally D. MOYNIHAN AND N. GLAZER, BEYOND THE MELTING POT (Cambridge, Mass.: MIT Press, 1963).

41. See NOTES OF DEBATES IN THE FEDERAL CONVENTION OF 1787 AS REPORTED BY JAMES MADISON (1920; reprint, New York: Norton, 1969) 503–5; T. JEFFERSON, NOTES ON THE STATE OF VIRGINIA (1787; reprint, Chapel Hill: Univ. of North Carolina Press, 1955) 163; D. ROBINSON, SLAVERY IN THE STRUCTURE OF AMERICAN POLITICS (New York: Norton, 1979) 225–28.

42. W. L. N. Rose, Slavery and Freedom (New York: Oxford Univ. Press, 1982) 26–27; E. Foner, Politics and Ideology in the Age of the Civil War (New York: Oxford Univ. Press, 1980) 40–42.

43. D. Potter, The Impending Crisis 1848–1861 (New York: Harper & Row, 1976) 451–55; D. B. Davis, "The Emergence of Immediatism in British and American Antislavery Thought," in Antebellum Reform (D. B. Davis, ed.) (New York: Harper & Row, 1967) 150–51.

44. E. Foner, Free Soil, Free Labor, Free Men (New York: Oxford Univ. Press, 1970) 51–66, 301–13.

45. This was Stephen Douglas's view at the time. Potter, *supra* note 43, at 337–38. For a retrospective view, see G. Ramsdell, "The Natural Limits of Slave Extension," 16 Miss. Valley Hist. Rev. 151 (1929).

46. 60 U.S. (19 How.) 393 (1857).

47. See Foner, *supra* note 44, at 51–66.

48. D. Potter, Lincoln and His Party in the Secession Crisis (New Haven: Yale Univ. Press, 1942) 301, 321.

49. D. Potter, The South and Sectional Conflict (Baton Rouge: Louisiana State Univ. Press, 1968) 220.

50. *Id.* at 233–37.

51. *Id.* at 243–62.

52. Foner, *supra* note 44, at 25. See also P. Paludan, "The American Civil War Considered as a Crisis in Law and Order," 77 Amer. Hist. Rev. 1013 (1972).

53. See D. Rothman, The Discovery of the Asylum (Boston: Little, Brown, 1971).

54. If the ratio of dead to population had been the same as that of Southern dead to Southern population in the Civil War, five million Americans would have died in World War II rather than the 384,000 actually killed. T. Williams, "The Strange Sad War," in The Selected Essays of T. Harry Williams (Baton Rouge: Louisiana State Univ. Press, 1983) 31, 33.

55. See Potter, *supra* note 48, at 226–31.

56. See R. Wiebe, The Opening of American Society: From the Adoption of the Constitution to the Eve of Disunion (New York: Random House, Vintage Books, 1984) 321–75.

57. G. Frederickson, The Black Image in the White Mind (New York: Harper & Row, 1972) 165.

58. See FONER, *supra* note 42, at 51–66. Compare David Brion Davis's similar suggestion regarding the relationship of anti-slavery attitudes and changing patterns of labor relations in England. D. B. DAVIS, THE PROBLEM OF SLAVERY IN THE AGE OF REVOLUTION 1770–1823 (Ithaca, N.Y.: Cornell Univ. Press, 1975) 453–68. See also Tocqueville's observation, *supra* note 12, at 343, in the early 1830s:

> Race prejudice seems stronger in those states that have abolished slavery than in those where it still exists, and nowhere is it more intolerant than in those states where slavery was never known. . . . In the South the master has no fear of lifting the slave up to his level, for he knows that when he wants to he can always throw him down into the dust. In the North the white man no longer clearly sees the barriers that separate him from the degraded race, and he keeps the Negro at a distance all the more carefully because he fears lest one day they be confounded together.

59. See J. ROARK, MASTERS WITHOUT SLAVES (New York: Norton, 1977).

60. C. V. WOODWARD, THE STRANGE CAREER OF JIM CROW (New York: Oxford Univ. Press, 1957) 56–77.

61. See FONER, *supra* note 44, at 98; J. COOPER, THE WARRIOR AND THE PRIEST: WOODROW WILSON AND THEODORE ROOSEVELT (Cambridge, Mass.: Harvard Univ. Press, 1983) 115; BOYER, *supra* note 21, at 125–30.

62. FONER, *supra* note 42, at 29–38.

63. FONER, *supra* note 44, at 126–27; R. SENNETT, AUTHORITY (New York: Knopf, 1980) 62–77 (discussing the relationship of George Pullman to his workers before the 1894 strike, and the significance of Pullman's insistence that workers living in his "model company town" could not own their homes).

5. A Jewish Court

1. Gom Lum v. Rice, 275 U.S. 278 (1927), South Covington v. Kentucky, 252 U.S. 399 (1920).

2. Powell v. Alabama, 287 U.S. 45 (1932), Nixon v. Condon, 286

U.S. 73 (1932), Missouri ex. rel. Gaines v. Canada, 305 U.S. 337 (1938), Buchanan v. Worley, 245 U.S. 60 (1917).

3. Quoted in A. Lief, Brandeis: The Personal History of An American Ideal (New York: Stackpole Sons, 1936) 205.

4. L. Brandeis, "Our New Peonage: Discretionary Pensions," The Independent, 25 July 1912, at 73, reprinted in L. Brandeis, Business—A Profession (Boston: Small, Maynard, 1914) 71. For Holmes's more active disregard for the reality of Southern black peonage, see his dissent in Bailey v. Alabama, 219 U.S. 219, 246 (1911); see generally Y. Rogat, "Mr. Justice Holmes: A Dissenting Opinion" (Part II), 15 Stan. L. Rev. 254 (1963).

5. For Brandeis's more forthcoming observations regarding discriminatory treatment of Asian-Americans, see Wan v. United States, 266 U.S. 1 (1924), Strum, *supra,* chap. 2, note 5, at 333–34.

6. L. Brandeis, "The Living Law," 10 Illinois L. Rev. 461 (1916).

7. Brandeis, *supra* note 4.

8. See A. Paul, Conservative Crisis and the Rule of Law: Attitudes of Bar and Bench, 1887–1895 (Ithaca, N.Y.: Cornell Univ. Press, 1960) 83–88, 119–22.

9. See generally M. Silverstein, Constitutional Faiths: Felix Frankfurter, Hugo Black, and the Process of Judicial Decision Making (Ithaca, N.Y.: Cornell Univ. Press, 1984).

10. *Id.* at 198–99.

11. *Id.* at 152–53. The Frankfurter/Black dispute about textual interpretivism has recently re-emerged in constitutional law scholarship, pushed by the same social imperatives and pulled toward the same inevitably indeterminate results. Compare, e.g., R. Bork, "The Impossibility of Finding Welfare Rights in the Constitution," 1979 Wash. U. L. Q. 695, with M. Perry, The Constitution, the Courts, and Human Rights (New Haven: Yale Univ. Press, 1982).

12. Lochner v. New York, 198 U.S. 45, 56 (1905).

13. See Mendelson, *supra,* chap. 2, note 48, at 83.

14. In the 1969 term, the total number of words published in opinions by the justices was 374,000; in the 1972 term, this number had escalated to 1,044,000, and it has remained in this range. See G. Casper and R. Posner, The Workload of the Supreme Court (Chicago: Amer. Bar Fndn., 1976) 80; G. Casper and R. Posner, "The Caseload of the Supreme Court, 1975 and 1976 Terms," 1977

SUP. CT. REV. 87, 96; F. Easterbrook, "Agreement among the Justices: An Empirical Note," 1984 SUP. CT. REV. 389, 390.

15. See BICKEL, *supra,* chap. 2, note 45, at 221–22; S. Levinson, "The Democratic Faith of Felix Frankfurter," 25 STAN. L. REV. 430, 431 n.9.

16. Direct challenges to the legitimacy of judicial authority are more apparent on the Court itself, as evidenced by the increased unwillingness of individual justices to join in majority Court opinions. In the 1894 term there were only 18 dissents and no concurrences accompanying 188 Court majority opinions. In 1934 there were 13 dissents and 7 concurrences with 168 Court opinions. By contrast, in 1954 there were 46 dissents and 14 concurrences accompanying only 82 Court opinions; in 1964 the numbers were 60 dissents, 43 concurrences, and 12 mixed concurring/dissenting opinions accompanying 95 Court opinions; in 1974 it was 125 dissents, 54 concurrences, and 13 mixed opinions with 155 Court opinions. CASPER AND POSNER, *supra* note 14, at 80. In the 1984 term, the comparable figures were 101 dissents, 61 concurrences, and 15 mixed opinions with 148 Court opinions.

17. See generally R. KLUGER, SIMPLE JUSTICE (New York: Random House, Vintage Books, 1975).

18. See PAUL, *supra* note 8.

19. The five Roosevelt appointees who remained on the Court in 1954 were Justices Black, Reed, Frankfurter, Douglas, and Jackson.

20. Compare H. Monaghan, "Of 'Liberty' and 'Property,'" 62 CORNELL L. REV. 405 (1977).

21. The modern Court has itself expressed doubts about the good sense of distinguishing "economic" and "personal" rights. See Lynch v. Household Finance Corp., 405 U.S. 538, 552 (1972); Gunther, *supra,* chap. 2, note 59, at 37–40.

22. 163 U.S. 537 (1896).

23. P. Elman, "The Solicitor General's Office, Justice Frankfurter, and Civil Rights Litigation, 1946–1960: An Oral History," 100 HARV. L. REV. 817, 831 (1987) (discussing Brown v. Board of Education [*Brown II*], 349 U.S. 294 [1955]).

24. For such justification, see my article, "Constitutional Law and the Teaching of the Parables," 93 YALE L.J. 455, 485–86 (1984).

25. A. BICKEL, THE SUPREME COURT AND THE IDEA OF PROGRESS

(New York: Harper & Row, 1970) 6: "The listener would have noted persistent indications of Mr. Justice Jackson's feeling that the issue before the Court was better left to the legislature, and that the ideal solution of it from the Court's point of view would be to find a formula for making precisely a sort of 'abstract declaration' that would encourage Congress to deal with the problem."

26. *Ibid.*

27. Letter from Frankfurter to Harlan, 2 September 1958, quoted in D. O'BRIEN, STORM CENTER: THE SUPREME COURT IN AMERICAN POLITICS (New York: Norton, 1986) 278.

28. The Court did not abandon the "deliberate speed" formula until 1968, in Green v. New Kent County School Board, 391 U.S. 430 (1968). Until then the Court had left desegregation enforcement "largely to lower court litigation—and to the political process . . . [breaking] its silence only rarely, though firmly." G. GUNTHER, CONSTITUTIONAL LAW (Mineola, N.Y.: Foundation Press, 1980) (10th ed.) 766.

29. See Walker v. City of Birmingham, 388 U.S. 307 (1967), discussed in chapter 6, *infra*.

30. See R. Merton, "Insiders and Outsiders: A Chapter in the Sociology of Knowledge," 78 AM. J. SOCIOLOGY 9 (1972).

31. Frankfurter indirectly revealed his distaste for racially preferential affirmative action programs—a policy inconsistent with the ideal of a uniform assimilated social identity—in Hughes v. Superior Court, 339 U.S. 460 (1950), which upheld a state court prohibition on labor picketing for racially preferential hiring policies. Writing for the Court, Frankfurter stated (*id.* at 464):

> To deny California the right to ban picketing in the circumstances of this case would mean that there could be no prohibition of the pressure of picketing to secure proportional employment on ancestral grounds of Hungarians in Cleveland, of Poles in Buffalo, of Germans in Milwaukee, of Portuguese in New Bedford, of Mexicans in San Antonio, of the numerous minority groups in New York, and so on through the whole gamut of racial and religious concentrations in various cities. States may well believe that such constitutional sheltering [of picketing] would inevitably encourage use of picketing to compel employment on the basis of racial discrimination. In

disallowing such picketing States may act under the belief that otherwise community tensions and conflicts would be exacerbated. The differences in cultural tradition instead of adding flavor and variety to our common citizenry might well be hardened into hostilities by leave of law. The Constitution does not demand that the element of communication in picketing prevail over the mischief furthered by its use in these situations

32. 356 U.S. 86 (1958).
33. *Id.* at 101.
34. *Id.* at 101–2.
35. *Id.* at 110–11.
36. *Id.* at 124.
37. *Id.* at 127.
38. *Ibid.*
39. *Id.* at 122.
40. *Id.* at 101–2.
41. *Id.* at 110–11.
42. 347 U.S. at 494–95, n.11.
43. *Id.* at 494.
44. See School Dist. v. Schempp, 374 U.S. 203 (1963) (prohibiting state from requiring public school prayer).
45. See Watkins v. United States, 354 U.S. 178 (1957) (restricting congressional committee authority to inquire into Communist party affiliations).
46. See Miranda v. Arizona, 384 U.S. 436 (1966) (requiring warnings and appointed counsel for criminal suspects in custody).
47. See Griffin v. Illinois, 351 U.S. 12 (1956) (requiring free transcripts for appeals from criminal convictions).
48. See Levy v. Louisiana, 391 U.S. 68 (1968) (invalidating discrimination against illegitimate child in state wrongful death statute).
49. 381 U.S. 479 (1965).
50. See *supra,* chap. 2, notes 19–22 and accompanying text.
51. Poe v. Ullman, 367 U.S. 497 (1961).
52. 356 U.S. at 102.
53. Arendt, *supra,* chap. 4, note 1, at 296.
54. Comment, "The Expatriation Act of 1954," 64 Yale L.J. 1164, 1190 and n.139 (1955).

55. 239 F.2d 527, 530 (2d Cir. 1957).

56. 356 U.S. at 101 and n.33.

57. ARENDT, *supra,* chap. 4, note 1, at 295–96.

58. 356 U.S. at 127.

59. Dred Scott v. Sandford, 60 U.S. (19 How.) 393 (1857).

60. 356 U.S. at 128.

61. Compare Holmes's observation, "In my epitaph they ought to say, 'here lies the supple tool of power.'" Quoted in Rogat, *supra,* chap. 2, note 47, at 249–50.

62. Quoted in BAKER, *supra,* chap. 2, note 31, at 393–94. Frankfurter's protestations of disbelief were not merely rhetorical; he did not use his access to President Roosevelt to convey Karski's allegations about Nazi genocide or to express concern generally about the concentration camps. See D. WYMAN, THE ABANDONMENT OF THE JEWS: AMERICA AND THE HOLOCAUST, 1941–1945 (New York: Pantheon, 1984) 316, 412.

6. Priests and Prophets

1. The text of King's speech appears as Appendix B to the opinion of the Court in Walker v. City of Birmingham, 388 U.S. 307, 323–24 (1967).

2. 388 U.S. 307 (1967).

3. 330 U.S. 258, 308–9 (1947).

4. 388 U.S. at 320–21.

5. Thus King stated that he was not "attempt[ing] to evade or defy the law," and that he "risk[ed] this critical move with an awareness of the possible consequences involved." 388 U.S. at 324.

6. 388 U.S. at 321.

7. *Id.* at 349.

8. See D. GARROW, BEARING THE CROSS: MARTIN LUTHER KING, JR., AND THE SOUTHERN CHRISTIAN LEADERSHIP CONFERENCE (New York: William Morrow, 1986) 481–97.

9. 356 U.S. 86, 99 (1958).

10. Witherspoon v. Illinois, 391 U.S. 510, 520 (1968).

11. 391 U.S. at 520 n.17, quoting ARTHUR KOESTLER, REFLECTIONS ON HANGING (London: Gollancz, 1956) 166–67.

12. M. Meltsner, Cruel and Unusual: The Supreme Court and Capital Punishment (New York: Random House, 1973) 30–31.
13. *Id.* at 123–27.
14. 408 U.S. 238 (1972).
15. *Id.* at 290.
16. *Id.* at 309.
17. *Id.* at 309–10.
18. Gregg v. Georgia, 428 U.S. 153 (1976), Profitt v. Florida, 428 U.S. 242 (1976), Jurek v. Texas, 428 U.S. 262 (1976), Woodson v. North Carolina, 428 U.S. 280 (1976), Roberts v. Louisiana, 428 U.S. 325 (1976).
19. 391 U.S. at 520 n.17.
20. 391 U.S. at 520.
21. Gregg v. Georgia, 428 U.S. 153, 179 (1976).
22. *Id.* at 183.
23. *Ibid.*, citing Furman v. Georgia, 408 U.S. at 308.
24. 388 U.S. at 321.
25. Compare the concern about vigilantism, mob violence, and anarchy that was at the core of Lincoln's willingness to unleash violence to preserve the Union, discussed in text accompanying chap. 4, notes 52–53, *supra*.
26. 388 U.S. at 321, 408 U.S. at 308.
27. See Arendt, *supra,* chap. 4, note 1, at 311–23.
28. Whitney v. California, 274 U.S. 357, 375 (1927).
29. *Id.* at 379.
30. *Id.* at 376.
31. Duplex Printing Press Co. v. Deering, 254 U.S. 443 (1921).
32. *Id.* at 486.
33. *Id.* at 488.
34. Bickel, *supra,* chap. 2, note 45.
35. Mason, *supra,* chap. 2, note 1, at 443.
36. *Ibid.*
37. *Ibid.*
38. Strum, *supra,* chap. 2, note 5, at 230.
39. *Ibid.*
40. De Haas's account was that, as Brandeis accompanied him to the train station, he "ventured to identify the Boston attorney with the Louisville uncle for whom he [Brandeis] was named. Brandeis's

admission came readily enough, and upon repetition of the sentence 'Louis N. Dembitz was a noble Jew,' there was instant demand for explanation of that term." J. DE HAAS, *supra,* chap. 2, note 9, at 51. De Haas stated that this conversation occurred in 1910, but Brandeis's later, more detailed recollection of a 1912 meeting suggests that De Haas mistakenly conflated his initial brief meeting with Brandeis in 1910 and the subsequent more fateful encounter in 1912.

41. MASON, *supra,* chap. 2, note 1, at 27.

42. Brandeis told his cousin Josephine Goldmark, "My uncle, the abolitionist, was a lawyer, and to me nothing else seemed really worth while." GOLDMARK, *supra,* chap. 2, note 4, at 286.

43. THE WORDS OF JUSTICE BRANDEIS (Solomon Goldman, ed.) (New York: Henry Schuman, 1953) 160.

44. REMINISCENCES OF FREDERIKA DEMBITZ BRANDEIS (trans. Alice G. Brandeis) (privately printed, 1943) 47.

45. *Id.* at 32–33.

46. *Id.* at 28.

47. *Id.* at 34.

48. *Id.* at 3.

49. Warren and Brandeis, *supra,* chap. 2, note 20, at 196.

50. Brandeis, letter of 10 July 1919. Quoted in MASON, *supra,* chap. 2, note 1, at 457.

51. Brandeis, quoted in UROFSKY, *supra,* chap. 2, note 10, at 92.

52. Frederika Brandeis, *supra* note 44, at 16, 20, 22, 29–30, 32.

53. BICKEL, *supra,* chap. 2, note 45, at 221–22.

54. See generally MURPHY, *supra,* chap. 3, note 2.

55. As Holmes wrote to Brandeis in 1919, "Generally speaking, I agree with you in liking to see social experiments tried but I do so without enthusiasm because I believe it is merely shifting the pressure and that so long as we have free propagation Malthus is right in his general view." Quoted in BICKEL, *supra,* chap. 2, note 45, at 221.

56. Judith Shklar has suggested generally that such tension, such conviction of inauthenticity, results from social mobility and the "anguish of people who leave the social world of their childhood behind them and adopt new manners and roles." She continues: "The true inner self is identified with one's childhood and family, and regret as well as guilt for having left them behind may render new ways artificial, false, and in some way a betrayal of that original self. This

personal self is seen as having a primacy that no later social role can claim. . . . Snobbery becomes a troubling fact of life, as does the sense of self-betrayal." J. SHKLAR, ORDINARY VICES (Cambridge, Mass.: Harvard Univ. Press, 1984) 75–76. H. N. Hirsch in his psychological study specifically characterizes Frankfurter as plagued by a personal sense of inauthenticity, though Hirsch frames this characterization in a cumbersome model adapted from the work of Karen Horney that obstructs more than it advances his presentation. H. HIRSCH, THE ENIGMA OF FELIX FRANKFURTER (New York: Basic Books, 1981) 5–10, 201–10.

57. See *supra,* chap. 3, notes 40–41 and accompanying text.

58. MASON, *supra,* chap. 2, note 1, at 72.

59. DIARIES, *supra,* chap. 3, note 1, at 14.

60. See M. WALZER, EXODUS AND REVOLUTION (New York: Basic Books, 1985) 43–45, 52–55.

61. *Id.* at 55.

62. *Id.* at 91.

63. For an account of one instance of this turning away, see J. RIEDER, CANARSIE: THE JEWS AND ITALIANS OF BROOKLYN AGAINST LIBERALISM (Cambridge, Mass.: Harvard Univ. Press, 1985).

64. I have explored this proposition at greater length in my article, "Constitutional Law and the Teaching of the Parables," 93 YALE L.J. 455 (1984).

65. See, e.g., Wainright v. Witt, 105 S.Ct. 844 (1985) (adopting more permissive standards and limiting appellate review for jury exclusions of death penalty opponents); Pulley v. Harris, 104 S.Ct. 871 (1984) (refusing to require state proportionality review of death sentences); Barefoot v. Estelle, 103 S.Ct. 3383 (1983) (liberalizing standards for summary affirmances of death penalty cases in federal appellate proceedings); Barclay v. Florida, 103 S.Ct. 3418 (1983) (liberalizing "harmless error" standards for federal court review of erroneous state impositions of death sentences). See also my article, "Disorder in the Court: The Constitution and the Death Penalty," 86 MICHIGAN L. REV. (forthcoming, 1987).

Index

Compositor: G&S Typesetters, Inc.
Text: 10/12 Bembo
Display: Bembo
Printer: Halliday Litho
Binder: Halliday Litho

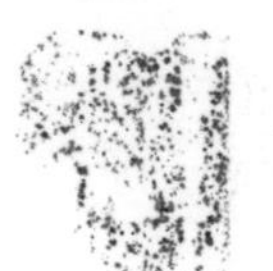